BITCOIN

THE ONLY BITCOIN INVESTING BOOK YOU'LL EVER
NEED: AN ABSOLUTE BEGINNER'S GUIDE TO THE
CRYPTOCURRENCY WHICH IS CHANGING THE
WORLD AND YOUR FINANCES IN 2021 AND BEYOND

FREEMAN PUBLICATIONS

CONTENTS

HOW TO PROFIT FROM CRYPTO IN THE STOCK MARKET

Whenever you have a paradigm shifting technology like cryptocurrency and blockchain… there is always more than one way to profit from it.

But before you rush out and buy every altcoin under the sun… there is a smarter way of doing this.

The way that hedge funds and Billionaire investors are using to make massive profits from the price of Bitcoin and other cryptocurrencies.

And you don't need anything more than a regular brokerage account to do so.

I covered exactly how to do this in a private call for our premium members recently.

But I thought it would be incredibly useful for you as well as you read this book.

So I uploaded the full recording of the call titled **4 "Backdoor" Ways to Profit from Cryptocurrency In The Stock Market**

Here's just a fraction of what we covered on the call

- The truth about GBTC
- **The "crypto bank" stock with the power to turn $1,000 into $20,000 or more**
- The 3 best blockchain ETFs

You can watch the recording of that call, plus get access to 8 other bonuses for free by going to https://freemanpublications.com/bonus

HOW TO GET THE MOST OUT OF THIS BOOK

To help you along your investing journey, we've created a free bonus companion course that includes spreadsheets, bonus video content, and additional resources that will help you get the best possible results. For this book in particular, we have a number of Bitcoin tutorials in the Bitcoin 101 section.

We highly recommend you sign up now to get the most out of this book. You can do that by going to the link below

https://freemanpublications.com/bonus

Free bonus #1: Company Valuation 101 video course ($97 value)

In this 8-part video course, you'll discover our process for accurately valuing a company. This will help you determine if a stock is overvalued, correctly valued, or a bargain, and give you an indication for when and if to buy it.

Free bonus #2: Guru Portfolios Analyzed ($37 value)

In these videos, we analyze the stock portfolios of Billionaire investors like Warren Buffett as well as top entrepreneurs like Bill Gates.

Free bonus #3: 2 Stocks to Sell Right Now ($17 value)

These 2 stocks are in danger of plummeting in the next 12 months. They are both popular with retail investors, and one is even in the top 5 most held stocks on Robinhood. Believe us; you do not want to be holding these in 2021 and beyond.

Free bonus #4: AI Disruptor - The $4 Stock Poised to be the Next Big Thing in Computing ($17 value)

This under-the-radar company, which less than 1% of investors have heard of, is at the forefront of a breakthrough technology that will change our lives as we know them. Soon, this technology will be in every smartphone, tablet and laptop on the planet.

Free bonus #5: Options 101 ($17 Value)

Options don't have to be risky. In fact, they were invented to *reduce* risk. It's no wonder that smart investors like Warren Buffett regularly use options to supplement their long-term portfolio. In this quick-start guide, we show you how options work and why they are tools to be utilized rather than feared.

Free bonus #6: The 1 Dividend Stock to Buy and Hold for the Rest of Your Life ($17 Value)

Dividends are the lifeblood of any income investor, and this stock is the cornerstone of any dividend strategy - a true dividend aristocrat with consistent payouts for over 50 years, which you'll surely want to add to your portfolio.

Free bonus #7: Top 3 Growth Stocks for 2021 ($17 Value)

Our 2020 selections outperformed the S&P 500 by 154%. Now we've released our top 3 picks for 2021.

Free bonus #8: Bitcoin 101 ($17 Value)

How to safely buy and store Bitcoin, even if you're a complete beginner. Contains video walkthroughs of everything you need for a stress free Bitcoin experience.

All of these bonuses are 100% free, with no strings attached. You don't need to provide any personal details except your email address.

To get your bonuses, go to:

https://freemanpublications.com/bonus

WHY BITCOIN? WHY NOW?

Investment allocation has always been a challenging task. There are so many asset classes out there that it can be hard to identify the best fit for your hard-earned cash.

Since 2008, Bitcoin and cryptocurrency have made waves as alternative assets of the future. Bitcoin in particular was the first cryptocurrency that emerged from the ashes of the 2008 financial crisis.

While its original premise was to provide individuals with an alternative and decentralized financial framework, it is safe to say that Bitcoin has moved beyond the initial vision that its founder had. Today, Bitcoin is all over the news. With the currency hitting new highs almost every other week, many investors have been wondering whether it makes sense to invest in it.

Our stance on this topic hasn't changed from our previous works. In our earlier book, *Bear Market Investing Strategies,* we noted that Bitcoin is a great alternative asset to hedge U.S. Dollar fluctuations. We also recommended investing no more than 10% of your portfolio into it.

Bitcoin's recent price appreciation hasn't changed our views. You can hedge your portfolio against a broad financial collapse while benefiting from price appreciation in the meantime.

Bitcoin has been around long enough for us to draw intelligent conclusions around its behavior as an asset. Our experience with it dates back to 2013, and cryptocurrency has experienced a wild ride since, to say the least. First, let's look at two of the main issues that investors have had with Bitcoin in the past.

VOLATILITY

Mention Bitcoin to any seasoned investor and the first thing you'll hear about is volatility. There's no denying that Bitcoin is far more volatile than any other asset classes. The price fluctuations in Bitcoin make the stock market look like a leisurely stroll through the park. If you've invested all of your money in stocks thus far, that might sound like a scary statement. However, as we will outline in this book, volatility isn't a reason for you to fear Bitcoin.

We will expand on methods and strategies you can use to hedge your portfolio against volatility while still benefiting from the positive qualities that Bitcoin brings to the table. It is worth noting several incidents that have eroded investor confidence throughout Bitcoin's history, as well as the lessons we can learn from them.

When Bitcoin first appeared on the scene, it was primarily used as a means of buying illegal drugs and laundering money. Unfortunately, this perception still remains despite illegal activity having decreased massively since then.

This initial wave of illicit activity fueled the premature hysteria around Bitcoin. When it first hit $1,000 in November of 2013, there was much rejoicing followed by shock as it plummeted 90% over the next few days. There was a lot of talk about whether Bitcoin was overrated or even safe.

Investors who stuck with Bitcoin back then soon found themselves dealing with another crisis. Mt. Gox, a major cryptocurrency exchange that handled over 70% of Bitcoin transactions worldwide, suffered a hack and lost close to 850,000 Bitcoin. Most of these coins have still not been recovered. However, that wasn't the end for Bitcoin.

2017 saw another seismic Bitcoin event when the currency hit $5,000 and kept climbing. This time, obscure cryptocurrencies known as "altcoins" gained 1,000% in a matter of a few days as well. It seemed as if everybody was jumping onto the cryptocurrency wagon. The crypto broker Coinbase became the most downloaded app on Google and Apple app stores. Euphoria drove the price up to a shocking $19,800, but this was followed by a crash that pushed Bitcoin all the way back down to mid $3,000s.

During 2020 Bitcoin had another resurgence and even touched $40,000 at the time of writing. We won't deny that there's a lot of irrational exuberance surrounding it, however, our perspective isn't informed by such emotions. We've witnessed Bitcoin rise and fall over time and aren't the least bit bothered by public speculations.

Our approach is still grounded in sound investment principles and we are looking at investing in Bitcoin from this perspective. It is definitely going to be a turbulent ride for investors. However, we must also note that Bitcoin is still in its second or third inning. There's a long way to go yet.

If you think there isn't much more room to grow, just remember that less than 10% of Americans own Bitcoin and around 1.5% of the worldwide population. In fact, a 2020 study by Blockworks (Redman,

2020) found that if you own more than 0.28 Bitcoin (around $14,000 at the time of writing), you are in the top 1% of all Bitcoin owners. Meaning there is still a lot of time for public adoption.

LEGITIMACY

The second recurring point in the Bitcoin debate is whether it should be considered a legitimate currency or not. What was once considered a currency that only drug dealers were be interested in has far more legitimacy today, thanks to financial institutions and famous investors piling into it.

The list of noteworthy financial names who have moved assets into Bitcoin is significant:

- Mexican Billionaire Ricardo Pliego invested 10% of his liquid portfolio in Bitcoin, according to Crypto Shields Against Wealth Expropriation
- Paul Tudor Jones has 2% of his assets in Bitcoin and is investing a portion of his funds' assets in it as an inflation hedge
- Elon Musk declared Bitcoin as "brilliant" in 2019, although he personally owns just 0.25 Bitcoin
- Internet pioneer and venture capitalist Tim Draper, who has funded companies like Baidu, Hotmail, Tesla, DocuSign and Robinhood, owns more than 30,000 Bitcoin (approximately $900 million at the time of writing)
- Chamath Palihapitiya, the CEO of Silicon Valley fund Social Capital has owned Bitcoin since 2012 and stated that he believes the cryptocurrency will hit $1m before 2037. Palihapitiya has also stated that everyone should have 1% of their assets in cryptocurrency.

It isn't just noteworthy investors who are moving money into Bitcoin. Devere Group, a wealth management firm, surveyed 700 of their high-net-worth clients and reported that 68% of them had either invested in Bitcoin or were going to invest by 2022. As far as we're concerned, there is no doubt that you should move a portion of your portfolio into Bitcoin. Doing this intelligently and according to sound investment principles is what this book is all about.

We must make it clear once again that we don't recommend putting 100% of your money into Bitcoin. That would be extremely foolish. We also don't recommend "diversifying" your portfolio by buying obscure altcoins in the name of reducing risk, or buying and trading cryptocurrency if you have never bought stocks or financial instruments previously.

Investing in Bitcoin isn't for everyone. As we've already outlined in our previous books, a lot depends on your temperament as an investor. Our objective is to describe the way this asset behaves and the qualities an ideal Bitcoin investor should have. Your job is to evaluate whether this applies to you. There is nothing wrong in choosing to pass on a Bitcoin investment. After all, FOMO is never a good motivation to make investment choices.

Keep this in mind as you read this book. Do not evaluate Bitcoin from the perspective of someone who's going to miss out if you don't put money into it "right now." Bitcoin is best bought as a part of a balanced portfolio. So, without further ado, let's dive right into the key things you need to know about Bitcoin.

FREEMAN BITCOIN INVESTING RULE #1

NEVER LET FOMO DRIVE YOUR DECISIONS

1

A HISTORY OF BITCOIN IN 10 MINUTES

To truly know an asset, you need to understand where it came from. Evaluating the history of an asset is critical if you want to understand how it works and why it behaves the way it does. It also makes deciding whether you want to invest in it simple. Understanding the history of Bitcoin simplifies how the cryptocurrency behaves and teaches you to use this knowledge to make better investment decisions.

ORIGIN

Bitcoin first appeared in 2009 as many parts of the world were still recovering from the 2008 financial crisis. While many crises in the past had exposed faults in the financial system, the 2008 crisis was unique in that it highlighted the divisions between the wealthy and the underprivileged in a stark manner. "Occupy" protests soon erupted, targeting corrupt bankers and the lawmakers who assisted them in designing an unequal financial system.

The average consumer realized, perhaps for the first time, that the deck was stacked against them unless they were in a position of privilege. Government programs weren't amounting to much and all public discourse was directed at how America wasn't about providing equal opportunity anymore. The subsequent bailouts that investment banks received only heightened the perception that the poor were being robbed to pay the rich.

The U.S. Government was the first to enact quantitative easing (QE) policies, which was a fancy term for printing money. While governments in the past had printed money with varying degrees of success, the world had never witnessed printing on the scale that began in 2008. Successive Western governments followed suit, and the money they printed was used to once again buy the toxic assets that banks had originally bought.

The effect of printing money *en masse* took a while to come to the surface. The most obvious effect was inflation. Inflation is an economic phenomenon where the prices of goods in an economy gradually increase. Inflation by itself isn't bad; it is the rate of inflation that matters. In a developed economy like the United States, a low rate of inflation (around one to two percent) is normal and wages can keep pace with it. Therefore, even as things get costlier, people don't suffer from reduced buying power because their wages increase at the same rate.

Growing economies, such as those of India and China in 2008, experience higher rates of inflation, but this is also normal. For example, India's inflation rate has routinely hovered around seven to eight percent since its economy began expanding. However, thanks to wages rising at the same rate or at faster rates, people could still afford goods and services.

The problem occurs when inflation outpaces the rate of wage increases. This results in hyperinflation where a normal rate of inflation becomes a runaway freight train that never stops. Hyperinflation occurs when people cannot afford the prices of goods and services and public unrest begins to form. Revolution or political change is usually the result of hyperinflation. The economies of Venezuela and Zimbabwe experienced these conditions where moderate inflation increased as much as 79,600,000,000% due to the corrupt policies of those countries' respective leaders (Hank and Kwok, 2009).

On the other extreme, deflation, or price decreases over time, is also a tricky situation. Prices decreasing over time might sound like a good thing, but it also means that the size of the economy is shrinking. Imagine a failed business that doesn't sell enough goods to make a profit and, therefore, doesn't have enough cash on hand to buy more attractive merchandise that can bring potential profits. It's a slow death spiral and, eventually, the business will have to close up the shop.

Governments avoid deflation at all costs because preventing inflation from running amok is easier than reviving a dead economy. Quantitative Easing (QE) policies result in inflation and not deflation, which is why they were used during the 2008 crisis and didn't face much objection from leading economists or politicians. Anything that would tide over the pain the world was experiencing seemed like a good solution.

Aftermath

The problem with QE was that it was being used to buy toxic assets and made incompetent banks stronger. This meant more profits for the bankers and more bonuses for their executives. Investment banks such as Goldman Sachs that nearly went under during the crisis posted profits by the end of 2008 while the economy was still reeling

(Goyette, 2011). The fact that the U.S. Federal Reserve and the Treasury Department were staffed by former Goldman employees wasn't lost on the public.

Thus, the benefits of QE were directed towards those who were already rich while small businesses and low-wage workers suffered job losses and foreclosures. Banks were bailed out for buying bad mortgages, but ordinary people were not bailed out by banks for drawing those same mortgages. The government turned a blind eye to the plight of these people, and it was clear that the financial system needed an overhaul.

Mere protesting wasn't enough. What the world needed was a complete overhaul of the way money worked and how it flowed through economies. Given the fact that governments were printing money as they pleased, the very nature of money was being questioned. After all, it was just a piece of paper that everyone collectively agreed represented a legal tender. What if everybody decided to stop treating a dollar bill as an acceptable form of currency?

While these economic debates about fiat (paper) currency were going on, technology was increasing at a rapid rate. Facebook became the face of social networking and Twitter was beginning to take its place as the internet's most opinionated platform. Programmers and developers around the world were beginning to explore the power of the internet and were inventing new protocols almost every day.

Old technologies that were once confined to research papers were now a reality thanks to the leaps that technology infrastructure was taking. The blockchain was an example of this. It was first proposed in a research paper back in 1998 as a way of creating more secure transactions. It became a reality, and a true game changer only in 2009. Blockchain leveraged the power of the internet to provide individuals on a network a completely different way of exchanging information.

Here's a simple explanation of how Blockchain technology works:

Let's say you wanted to send someone a document by email. You send it from your email address (which is proof of your identity) to their email address (proof of their identity) and attach the document. The other person views the document and verifies whether it's what they want. If the document is good, they thank you for it and move on. If not, they request changes.

The problem here is that the network over which you send the email with the document is controlled by someone else. For example, you use a Gmail account. If Google decides to shut down your account, you need to use another service. Now imagine if Google decided to tell every other email service provider not to give you an account. You'd have no way of using email.

There's also the issue that Google knows who you're sending information to and collects data on it, despite having nothing to do with the transaction. The document receiver also has an issue in that they need to rely solely on their judgment to verify the contents of the document. What if they're wrong? Or what if they slip up and make a mistake? They're stuck with useless information.

Replace the word "Google" with that of your bank and "document" with money and you have an illustration of how the traditional financial system works. Banks demand all kinds of information from senders and receivers, and have complete control over and access to your money. Banks and governments can easily shut down your access to your money if they so decide.

While this may sound completely dystopian if you live in the US or Western Europe, this scenario isn't far-fetched in countries led by despotic regimes. In fact, this is pretty much what Venezuela did to its citizens when hyperinflation meant people couldn't afford food or water. They banned people from exchanging their pesos to dollars and cracked down on anyone storing gold or alternative forms of wealth. India underwent a similar incident with the 2016 banknote demonetization and Lebanon is currently undergoing a crisis with its own currency with inflation now over 100%.

Controlling the financial system in this centralized manner also allows regimes to curb dissent. Political opponents can be muzzled if they don't have the money to carry out their agendas. Centralized financial systems give governments the authority to take your money as they please.

This isn't a scenario that pertains to despotic government alone. It also happens in the United States. Fall behind on your taxes and the IRS has the authority to directly withdraw any cash you might have, even if it isn't enough to pay your tax bill (*IRS Bank Levies Can Take Your Money*, 2014). If your bank allows overdrafts, the IRS will push your account into overdraft to get its money. The bank will then hit you with overdraft fees and penalize you even further. The U.S. Government also has a prior history in restricting private gold ownership, going so far as to put a complete ban on it that remained in effect from 1933 to 1974.

Centralized financial systems ensure that it becomes expensive to be poor. Your financial history is known to everybody and every time you approach a bank to borrow money to pay for an asset, it will cost you more if you have poor credit. People who have money and better credit literally find it cheaper to survive. They don't have to pay fees and additional interest. This is how the rich get richer while the poor remain where they are.

Satoshi Nakomoto

As people around the world woke up to the reality of a centralized financial system, a whitepaper appeared on the website *metzdowd.com* in October 2008. It was titled "Bitcoin: A Peer-to-Peer Electronic Cash System" and it was authored by someone named Satoshi Nako-moto. To this day, no one knows who this person is or even if it is a single individual or a group of people.

The whitepaper outlined an idea of using the blockchain to exchange money. Going back to our previous example, here is how the system would work. Money would be exchanged over a network where neither the sender nor the receiver would know one another's identi-ties. Instead, they would know each other only by their addresses on the network which would be represented by a string of 26-35 alphanumeric characters.

The network itself would not be controlled by a single entity but by everyone present on it. The details of the transaction would be vali-dated by everyone else on the network so the receiver could rest assured that everything was in order. As for the money itself, it was called Bitcoin and would be created when a computer solved a complex algorithm.

We will shortly explain how Bitcoin is created. For now, we will just say that using a revolutionary technology (blockchain) to transfer money opened up the possibility of a new financial order. Revolution was in the air following the behavior of governments and banks in the aftermath of 2008 and people were ready to adopt the idea of a parallel financial system.

It created quite a splash, but people struggled to understand how blockchain worked and how Bitcoin was created. This confusion persists to this day and is why we've written this book. Bitcoin was enthusiastically adopted by cryptography evangelists and cyberanar-chists who saw the benefits of overthrowing the current centralized financial system. It was a way to even the odds again.

The first ever Bitcoin transaction occurred on January 12th 2009, when Satoshi Nakamoto sent 10 Bitcoin to computer programmer Hal Finney. With the first USD dollar/Bitcoin transaction occurring in 2010 when a developer named Laszlo Hanceyz exchanged 10,000 Bitcoin for US dollars (at a market price of roughly $40) so he could order pizza for his family.

Figure 1: Laszlo Hanceyz's original pizza post on the cryptocurrency forum Bitcointalk

Although Hanceyz has since stated he doesn't regret the transaction, because he helped kickstart real world use cases for Bitcoin, today his 10,000 Bitcoin would be worth approximately $38 million. That's one expensive pizza!

It should also be said that Hanceyz was one of the earliest adopters of Bitcoin, and even wrote some of the code used in today's mining algo-rithm. Many of those original Bitcoin believers are deeply uncomfort-able about the way Bitcoin's price has risen. They can see that the price appreciation is primarily due to people looking to make money instead of believing in the cause. While their views might be a bit utopian, there's no denying that early Bitcoin adopters contributed a lot to where the cryptocurrency is today and many of them have been compensated massively for it.

HOW BITCOIN WORKS

There are a few other important points that make Bitcoin a noteworthy asset. Its digital nature makes it tough to understand but the process by which it is generated, stored, and transferred is quite simple once you grasp the basics. Let's begin by looking at how it's created or "mined."

Mining

Bitcoin exists on the blockchain, which is a network of computers. Every computer on the network can create or mine Bitcoin. Mining in this context isn't a bunch of soot-faced, sweaty men diving deep under the earth. Mining Bitcoin is all about solving cryptographic problems. These problems are mathematical in nature and require considerable resources to solve.

A computer adds a new block to the chain once it solves a problem. This new block is worth a certain amount of Bitcoin. However, before the new block can be added to the network or chain, the rest of the network has to validate the solution. Practically speaking, if 51% of the network validates that the solution is correct, Bitcoin is awarded to the miner and the new block becomes a part of the chain.

Note that two miners can compete to solve the same problem. The miner that has greater resources usually ends up solving the problem faster and mines more Bitcoin. The fact that the majority of the network has to validate the transaction makes fraud nonexistent. This has to do with the nature of the blockchain itself and not Bitcoin. Think of Bitcoin as an app that rests on the operating system that is blockchain, much like how your web browser operates on the OS on your computer or cellphone.

How much Bitcoin do you get if you add a block to the network? Well, this is where Nakamoto's protocols are ingenious. The reward rate determines how much Bitcoin a miner receives. This rate has been decreasing over time. What's more, the number of blocks that can be mined or created are fixed. The result is there will be a finite number of bitcoin when the mining limit is reached. Also, as time goes on, thanks to the reward rate decreasing, miners will receive less Bitcoin for the blocks they add.

Bitcoin's reward rate is cut in half every 210,000 blocks (Borate, 2021). In terms of time, this means the reward rate halves every four years. The reasoning behind introducing the reward rate halving algorithm is that the supply of bitcoin remains steady. As more people join the network, the rewards diminish, and the number of coins doesn't change by too much. This prevents the value of existing Bitcoin from bottoming out.

When Bitcoin first arrived on the scene, a regular household computer could mine a single coin within a few hours. These days, it takes an extremely powerful supercomputer approximately 14 days to mine a block (Borate, 2021).

As of November 2020, the reward per block was 6 coins. At current prices, mining Bitcoin is certainly worth it. However, if it dips below the costs associated with the mining process, even the most optimized mining setups would be better off buying coins on an exchange.

Transaction Verification

Since all transactions occur on a network, you might think that information is visible to everyone on it. This is partly true. Information regarding the amount of Bitcoin (abbreviated to BTC from henceforth) transferred is public. However, personal information about either party involved in the transaction is private. This means BTC transactions carry a high degree of anonymity. Figure 1 illustrates the way a normal BTC transaction appears:

Figure 2: A sample Bitcoin transaction, publicly visible on the blockchain

BTC operates and stores transactions on what is called an open-source, public ledger. Open-source refers to the nature of the BTC blockchain itself. Network information is public, and any developer can become a part of the team that is tasked with maintaining it. Improvements to the network and new algorithms to enhance it are announced publicly for the entire community to review.

In fact, many altcoins have "forked" or created a new path from the BTC blockchain to birth new alternative currencies. When analyzing BTC on a technical level, there's no doubt that there are several things that could be improved. For example, despite anonymizing transaction party information, the BTC blockchain still reveals a lot of information about the parties involved. Alternative currencies such as Monero and Dash have forked from the main BTC blockchain to create currencies that offer greater degrees of privacy.

However, a lack of complete privacy shouldn't deter you from investing in it. The privacy question is most pertinent to the crypto evangelist crowd. If you aren't one of them, as you're unlikely to be if you're reading this book, absolute anonymity shouldn't be a major concern for you.

Supply

One of the key factors that makes BTC such a reliable asset is its scarcity. BTC was created to be scarce right from the beginning, with a limit of only 21 million. With the decreasing reward rate system in place, the last BTC will be mined some time in 2140. Scarcity is a unique value driver in BTC's case and is what makes it tough to understand from an economic standpoint.

Going back to the first part of this chapter, you learned that fiat money is unlimited because governments can simply print more of it to bail themselves out of trouble. The premise of BTC was to create an alternate financial order and this is why scarcity was so important. It is the opposite of fiat currency in every possible way.

Scarcity also ensures that BTC will always have some value as an asset. While it's impossible to predict what a good price for it is, we can rest assured that it will never be worthless. Currently 18.5 million BTC have been mined. While we are quite close to the limit, the reward algorithm will ensure that the rate at which BTC is mined is decreased dramatically to last us another century.

There's another factor that contributes to BTC's scarcity: resources. Mining BTC these days requires an army of supercomputers that require power to run. There's also the fact that these computers aren't cheap to buy and assemble. This means the economic cost of mining BTC will exceed the value of the coin at some point. While the current price levels make BTC mining attractive, there are better bargains to be found mining altcoins.

Here's how the reward per block has changed over the years:

- The initial reward was 50 BTC per block – it was consistent from 2008 to 2012.

- The first halving occurred on November 29, 2012 – the reward was halved to 25 per block.
- The second halving occurred on July 9, 2016 – the reward was halved to 12 BTC per block.
- The third halving occurred on May 11, 2020 – the reward was halved to 6.25 BTC per block

The next halving is scheduled to take place in 2024. There are 30 further halvings that are scheduled to take place before BTC can no longer be mined, sometime around 2140.

Decentralized

One of the biggest value drivers of BTC is that it's completely decentralized. There is no central authority that governs its usage or controls transactions. Compare this to fiat money transactions where your bank or the country's central bank has ultimate authority over how you spend your money or transfer it.

A lot of these compliance controls are set in place to prevent money laundering, and it's true that BTC attracted its fair share of illegal activity during its initial days. However, public adoption has increased to the point where the percentage of illegal activity taking place is now thought to be much lower. As governments increasingly tighten the screws around their monetary policies, BTC is proving to be a lifesaver for people everywhere.

Consider the previous example of Venezuela, which eliminated alternative currency access for its citizens. During that crisis, many Venezuelans moved their cash into BTC to preserve some modicum of value. While access to BTC is still limited, their net worth has been preserved to a large extent.

The degree to which governments will stoop to achieve their own ends knows no bounds. A good example of this was the crackpot scheme that India's government cooked up in 2016. As a purported effort to combat undeclared income hoarding in the form of cash, the government declared certain banknote denominations to be illegal and replaced it with new tender overnight.

This meant Indian citizens had to deposit their old bank notes and exchange them for new ones. While exchanging the old tender, people had to explain their sources of income. In true government fashion, none of the banks were prepared ahead of time and ran out of their supply of new cash. People were restricted to using fixed cash limits and virtually no one had any change to hand over. The Prime Minister was busy crying at political rallies to garner sympathy from the public while rural India was decimated due to its reliance on informal cash lending.

To this day the Indian government has not provided any clarity on how BTC ought to be treated apart from issuing a blanket statement terming it "illegal." This hasn't deterred Indians from buying BTC, and the country reportedly has one of the most active user bases around the world (Sharma, 2020).

BTC gains a ton of value every time a government decides to display despotic behavior such as this. The promise of an alternative financial system began appealing to people in the West in 2008, but in many parts of the world, people had become accustomed to shoddy financial systems. BTC and other cryptocurrency, thanks to their decentralized formats, carries a lot of potential for these people.

This is why BTC demand is always assured. When combined with its built-in scarcity, there's no doubt that BTC will always retain some value, even if the exact number might be difficult to predict.

2

SO, IS BITCOIN MONEY?

The ultimate question that every investor asks of BTC is whether it can be treated as money or not. There are two ways of examining the answer to this question. The first is to use a simple analogy and say that BTC is a currency just like the Swiss Franc (CHF) is an alternative to the U.S. Dollar.

For many years now, investors have considered the Swiss Franc to be a bad weather currency. Whenever the U.S. Dollar or American economy hits a rough patch, investors pour money into the CHF and deposits rise. The combination of Swiss neutrality and a strong, easily understood, and transparent legal system makes it a good store for value.

The difference between the CHF and BTC is that the former is a centralized currency. It is subject to inflation and its supply is unlimited. This means it doesn't retain any value connected to its inherent nature (a piece of paper). BTC, on the other hand, functions partly like a currency and partly like an asset class, such as gold.

BTC has been rightly termed the new gold or "digital gold" by many observers. Like BTC, gold gains most of its value by being viewed as an alternative means of exchanging value. If the earth were to enter a complete economic meltdown, you can rest assured that gold will still be valued. After all, every person on the planet recognizes it and values it. This is why gold prices spike after disasters or economic crises.

However, there is a flaw in this comparison. Gold doesn't have inherent value thanks to its nature. It isn't useful in many industrial processes and its value is derived solely from people thinking it's valuable. BTC isn't quite the same in that it has value thanks to its intrinsic scarcity. Its presence on the blockchain also adds value due to increased security, unlike physical gold, which can be stolen.

Perhaps this is why BTC is hard for investors to understand. It's part currency and part asset. Think of it as being a more accessible and practical version of gold. If you were to walk around carrying bars of gold with you, there is a very high chance that you'll soon have to part from them, but the same would never happen with BTC.

THE NATURE OF MONEY

The second method of understanding the nature of BTC is getting to the bottom of what constitutes a currency or money. There have been many forms of money throughout human history but there are a few qualities that have been common with all of them. When analyzing whether BTC is money, examining its qualities with regards to these characteristics is helpful. This is exactly what crypto evangelist and former hedge fund manager Robert Breedlove tried to do.

Scarcity

One of the most important qualities of any form of money is scarcity. This refers to the ease with which it can be reproduced and originated. The scarcity of an object used as money is important because this ensures supply remains under control and the monetary value of individual units isn't diluted. For example, if everyone had the ability to mint money at home, the value of a dollar bill would decrease. If everyone was walking around with $100 in their pockets, the prices of everyday goods would readjust to reflect the new monetary reality. Cash buying power would decrease and money itself would be worthless.

Fiat money has artificial supply barriers installed thanks to governments guarding their mints zealously. Governments also install lengthy verification workflows before a decision is made to print more money. In the current financial climate, it might seem as if all it takes to print more money is a phone call from the Federal Reserve, but this isn't the case. There are deliberations by economists and fiscal policy experts within the government before the nod is given. The decision to print money has become an easier process today because of the unique economic conditions that have never been encountered before.

These conditions are rendering basic economic theories invalid and this is why traditional economics has no answer for this situation. It also means BTC has a valid case of being treated as money. BTC has limited supply built right into its network as we explained in the previous chapter. The reward algorithm also ensures BTC is hard to replicate. The cost of processing power will steadily increase until there is no value anymore in mining BTC. Even if speculative bubbles pushed the price of BTC to astronomical levels, the hard limit on the number of coins means scarcity is always present.

Divisibility

For money to be widely adopted, it needs to be divisible. Divisibility refers to the ease with which a single unit of money can be broken down into smaller units. For example, a dollar bill is extremely divisible. It can be broken down into 100 pennies, four quarters, 10 dimes, or any combination of these smaller units.

Divisibility is a key aspect to widespread adoption and is what helped human societies move beyond the barter system. For example, if someone wished to exchange 10 sacks of wheat for five goats, and if both parties had these goods in those quantities, a transaction was possible. However, if someone had only one goat and if the wheat seller insisted on receiving five goats at a minimum, there was no way of seeing the transaction through.

The lack of divisibility also explains why other forms of value storage such as gold and silver were eventually abandoned. Gold is extremely valuable, and it can be broken down only so much. Silver suffers from the same problem. The only way to tackle this issue is to affix minimum purchase quantities, but that doesn't lead to an efficient market.

Paper money was adopted because it was easy to create divisibility. All it takes to make paper money divisible is to print another number on the bill. Economies run smoothly and everyone's happy. In fact, even amidst the drastic economic consequences of hyperinflation, paper money remains divisible. If the price of a gallon of milk rises to $200, that amount can still be broken down into smaller chunks easily. Whether anyone would have money to afford milk at those prices is a different matter. Paper money is always easily divisible.

Bitcoin on the other hand, suffered from a perceived lack of divisibility. In the early days, when a single Bitcoin was worth less than $100, this wasn't much of an issue. As the value of a single coin rose, and as it became tougher to mine a single coin, there was a clear need to enforce divisibility on the currency.

To clear up that misconception, Bitcoin is divisible. In fact, every BTC is divisible to an eighth decimal value. This means one BTC can be broken down into units of 0.00000001 BTC. This unit is also called a satoshi. Another way of writing this is to say that a single BTC is worth 100,000,000 satoshis.

Divisibility also ensures that BTC miners can be rewarded in increments, as opposed to spending a lot of effort and receiving nothing in exchange unless they spend resources to mine a single coin. This also means that mining BTC is always rewarding and the currency will progress towards its hard limit no matter what.

Later on, in this book we'll explain a better way to reframe how you see Bitcoin's divisibility. This will help you truly understand the long-term potential of BTC as a legitimate currency.

Portability

Another key aspect of money is portability. Portability refers to the ease with which it can be carried around for use. Going back to the example of fiat money, it's extremely easy to carry and use. Pieces of paper add virtually no encumbrance to the things you normally carry. Additionally, the rise in digital banking and transactions has revolutionized the way we use fiat money and made it even more portable.

In contrast, an alternative store of value such as gold does not offer the same ease. It is not easy to carry gold bars or bricks around since they're heavy and will almost certainly attract attention. Even wearing gold draws unwanted attention, making it extremely hard to port. If gold was portable, we wouldn't need an armed detail to transport it from one place to another.

BTC, on the other hand, is even more portable than fiat money. All it takes to make BTC transactions is scanning a QR code that reflects your wallet's address. You can send and receive BTC with a simple scan making it extremely portable. Even if you have an electronic wallet, all it takes is an internet connection and the click of a button to transact in BTC.

Moreover, unlike fiat money, there are no unwanted intermediaries such as correspondent banks or other exchange houses earning a commission from your transactions. BTC is a peer-to-peer network and the commissions that are collected are used to maintain the integrity of the network.

Durability

Durability is a tough bar for all forms of money to pass. In fact, most historical forms of money, including paper money, don't pass this test. Durability refers to how easy or tough it is to destroy a form of currency. Paper money is not durable. A dollar bill is easy to carry, but if it's torn or burned, it has no value. In fact, some countries designate even just slightly torn bills useless.

To combat this issue, digital money was introduced in the form of credit and debit cards. These cards are certainly more durable, but they can be stolen, and fraudulent transactions can be carried out easily. BTC's durability is one of the reasons it's become as popular as it has.

It's tough to steal BTC. The few instances of BTC theft that have occurred, have been possible when attackers have gained access to a wallet's electronic key. We'll explain electronic keys in more detail later in this book. For now, all you need to know is that the key acts in the same way a combination lock does for your safe. It controls access to your BTC holdings.

As for the coins themselves, not only is it impossible to steal BTC without wallet access, but there is also no way of replicating them. A single BTC is as permanent as anything can get. This permanence has posed inconveniences for BTC holders in the past. Your wallet's key or passcode is the most important piece of information you hold. It connects your ownership to your coins. The Mt. Gox incident that we highlighted in the introduction remains the biggest instance of BTC being stolen. However, this theft was not a bank heist where robbers ran away with a ton of cash. Many BTC users stored their coins with Mt. Gox instead of in wallets of their own.

Thus, Mt. Gox owned the keys to their users' wallets, and due to security lapses, these keys were stolen. As a result, millions of BTC were removed and transferred to other addresses. Don't worry if this sounds overwhelming or confusing. Later on in this book, we will show you the optimal Bitcoin storage setup so you can ensure this never happens to you.

What this does mean is that if a Bitcoin holder loses their private key or forgets it, they can never gain access to their coins again. Coins that the user has been locked out of cannot be accessed by anyone else or used for any purpose. The nature of the blockchain ensures those coins remain in place.

Thus, the durability of BTC is extraordinary. It also means users of BTC need to adjust to a new model of thinking about money. They need to guard their keys more closely than the money itself. This isn't the case with paper money, where we don't care much about our wallets as much as we do about their contents. However, as far as economic principles go, BTC is about as durable as any currency can get.

Recognizability

The recognizability of a form of money is the most important factor in its widespread adoption. Take the US Dollar as an example, it is universally recognizable and most people intuitively know its exchange rate to other forms of money. There are two keys to monetary recognition: it should be identifiable and verifiable. Every BTC too, is readily identified with a unique address on the blockchain. All of your coins reside in a wallet that has a specific address.

The main difference in recognizability between fiat currency and Bitcoin is how widely accepted it is as a form of money. While adoption of Bitcoin is increasing every year, it still is nowhere near the level of fiat currency. For this reason alone, we can still consider this an early stage in Bitcoin's adoption journey.

Traits of Money	Gold	Fiat Currency	Bitcoin
Scarcity	Medium	Low	High
Divisibility	Low	Medium	High
Portability	Medium	High	High
Durability	High	Medium	High
Recognizability	Medium	High	Medium

Figure 3: Comparing different forms of currency against the 5 key currency factors

3

ANSWERING YOUR 10 MOST COMMON BITCOIN QUESTIONS

There are many questions out there about Bitcoin and the nature of the network it operates on. From all the questions we received from our email subscribers and Facebook Group members, here are the most commonly asked queries about Bitcoin and their answers.

1. WHY IS BITCOIN WORTH SO MUCH?

Bitcoin is a potentially game-changing financial asset and a wildly speculative technology being used in an era where it's extremely easy to speculate on financial instruments. Anyone can buy Bitcoin on Coinbase or Robinhood in a matter of minutes and this fuels price rises like never before. Long-term investment remains the best way of placing your money in assets, irrespective of these bubbles.

2. ISN'T BITCOIN TOO EXPENSIVE?

As we explained in the previous chapter, each Bitcoin can be broken up into 100 million individual units, which are called satoshis. Therefore, when purchasing Bitcoin, you do not have to buy a full coin. You can purchase $1 worth of Bitcoin if you'd like.

However a psychological phenomenon known as "price anchoring bias" leads us to see "Bitcoin at $30,000" as expensive. This is because, outside of Berkshire Hathaway class A shares (currently trading at $347,000), there is no stock market entity or currency which trades close to $30,000. Even gold, which has historically been looked at as an "expensive" asset, currently trades around $1,800/ounce.

A better way to frame this question would be: how much is 1,000 millibitcoin (also known as mBTC) or 0.001 BTC worth? And the answer to that is, if Bitcoin is priced at $38,000, 1 mBTC would be $38.

If Bitcoin becomes widely adopted as a monetary means of exchange, it's likely that prices will be displayed in mBTC rather than in BTC. Therefore, if you view the price of Bitcoin in terms of mBTC, or as $38 rather than $38,000, you will realize that Bitcoin, in fact, has not yet reached peak price and there is more room to grow.

FREEMAN BITCOIN INVESTING RULE #2

TO AVOID PRICE ANCHORING BIAS, THINK OF BITCOIN PRICES IN TERMS OF MBTC

3. WHAT IF "THEY" JUST CREATE MORE BITCOIN?

There is no "they." There is no central entity controlling it. Creating more Bitcoin would require 51% of all Bitcoin miners to agree and that is an incredibly unlikely scenario. If the miners agreed to creating more Bitcoin, they would be hurting their own abilities and profits.

4. CAN A GOVERNMENT JUST BAN BITCOIN?

Yes they can, in fact, some countries do.

- Algeria, Pakistan, Nepal and Ecuador are four countries that have done so.
- Other countries have banned financial institutions from dealing in it.
- Some countries like India have banned cryptocurrency trading altogether.

However, at this point, Bitcoin is too deeply entrenched in the international financial system for there to be a global ban. A ban now would involve shutting down trillions of dollars' worth of financial institutions, creating the largest black market the world has ever seen. Hence, governments prefer tolerate it in the short term and choose to profit from it in the form of tax revenue rather than ban it. Recently the U.S. Treasury acknowledged the growing importance of Bitcoin with an announcement that recognizing the legitimacy of Bitcoin-related transactions and investments.

Besides, the digital nature of Bitcoin and the fact that internet transactions make up more than 99% of Bitcoin volume, make it incredibly difficult to enforce any sort of widespread ban.

5. CAN I MINE BITCOIN ON MY COMPUTER?

While this is possible, you will spend more on electricity than you will make back in Bitcoin. A typical non-specialized laptop dedicated to mining Bitcoin will likely earn less than $1 worth of Bitcoin in a year, while spending hundreds of dollars on electricity.

A dedicated Bitcoin mining rig such as the Antminer S9 will set you back around $3,000. These rigs run at 14 TH/S, which will give you around 0.037 BTC per year (around $1,250 at today's prices). One TH/S stands for one trillion hashes per second whereas a hash is a measure of how much power the Bitcoin network is consuming to generate a block every 10 minutes. So, even if your Antminer was running 24/7, with the standard U.S. electricity cost of $0.12 per kilowatt/hour, your annual electricity cost is $1,422. That still leaves you with a loss of $172 per year.

And this is before you factor in other expenses such as the cost of the fans you will need to cool your mining rig in the summer and the additional electricity expenses this will bring. In short, if you live in the United States and don't have access to heavily subsidized electricity costs, then mining Bitcoin yourself will be total a waste of money.

The majority of Bitcoin mining today takes place in China because of cheaper electricity costs. There are also rumors that state-run Chinese utility companies have dedicated extra power towards Bitcoin mining.

There are also services which advertise "cloud mining." This is a service where you invest your Bitcoin in exchange for shares in the cloud mining companies' collective mining power. The vast majority of these companies are classic Ponzi schemes where new money is used to pay earlier investors and no actual mining is occurring. The largest one of these was the BitClub Network scam where four men took over $722 million worth of Bitcoin from investors in exchange for shares in a "cloud mining" operation which never existed (*Bitclub*, 2019).

FREEMAN BITCOIN INVESTING RULE #3

DO NOT TRY TO MINE BITCOIN ON YOUR HOME COMPUTER

6. CAN BITCOIN BE TRACED?

There is some confusion regarding Bitcoin's anonymity and what can and cannot be traced by a network. We'll start by reiterating the basics: with blockchain technology, every single Bitcoin transaction is public record. This includes all transactions on exchanges as well as private exchanges from wallet to wallet.

Each wallet has a unique address. This address is just a long string of numbers and letters, but each one is unique to a specific wallet. A sample address would look like this:

1BvBMSEYstWetqTFn5Au4m4GFg7xJaNVN2

If you're worried that you would have to remember an incredibly long string of numbers and letters, then take a breather. In practical terms, most wallet addresses are represented by QR codes that you can scan with a cellphone. This property of Bitcoin allows people to link wallets with real-world identities (Roberts, 2020).

For example, you send coins from your personal wallet to your exchange wallet. The wallet on the exchange could be linked to your identity because you most likely needed to prove your identity when you signed up to the exchange. If someone knows that, then they can assume that the wallet you transferred money from also belongs to you. Hence, while your name won't be broadcasted on the blockchain, your wallet address will be known to all.

7. CAN BITCOIN BE HACKED?

Another source of confusion regarding Bitcoin is whether it can be "hacked." Since its inception in 2009, the Bitcoin network has never been hacked. While this is possible in theory, it would take an enormous amount of computing power to hack the Bitcoin network. It would involve hacking the entire network and gaining more than 51% control. This would be a multi-billion-dollar operation to pull off, and there are very few bad actors with that kind of monetary backing, let alone the wherewithal to pull it off.

What does it mean when you see news articles relating stories about people's Bitcoin being "stolen"? This is because Bitcoin exchanges have been hacked in the past. The most famous example of this was the Mt. Gox incident, when hackers breached security protocols of the largest Bitcoin exchange in the world at the time with around 70% of the world's Bitcoin transactions taking place on it.

The hackers stole approximately 850,000 Bitcoin, or around four percent of the world's total supply. This was stolen from Mt. Gox's cryptocurrency wallet, which stored most of the customers' Bitcoin. The lesson here is to always store your Bitcoin outside of an exchange. We'll show you the easiest way to do this later in this book.

A secure hardware wallet for which only you know the private keys is impossible to hack. To put it simply, if you can trust the internet, you can trust the Bitcoin network.

8. CAN BITCOIN BE CONVERTED TO CASH?

Yes, you can liquidate your Bitcoin back to fiat currency by selling it on an exchange—the same way you purchased it.

9. WILL BITCOIN REACH $100,000/$1,000,000 OR THESE OTHER AUDACIOUS PRICE TARGETS I SEE ONLINE?

It may. It may not.

The current largest price prediction from a legitimate financial institution has Bitcoin potentially reaching a peak of $318,000 by December 2021. This was from a leaked report by Citibank titled "Bitcoin: 21st Century Gold" which was sent to a number of Citibank's high profile institutional clients (Lyanchev, 2020).

But let's look at what the implications of these large numbers would be. At the current price of $38,000, Bitcoin has a market cap of just over $700 billion. That's about the same as Alibaba and a little less than Tesla.

At $100,000 Bitcoin would have a market cap of $2.1 trillion. For reference, Apple's market cap at the time of writing was $2.26 trillion.

At $114,000, Satoshi Nakamoto, who holds an estimated 1.1 million BTC, would become the richest man in the world. (With Bitcoin at $114,000, Nakamoto's net worth would be approximately $124.4 billion.). This is assuming Satoshi Nakamoto is one person and not a group of people.

The world's aboveground gold reserves, which includes jewelry, private holdings, and official physical gold deposits are worth approximately $10.9 trillion (at a gold price of $1,800/ounce). At $500,000 per Bitcoin, it would represent roughly the same total market cap as aboveground gold reserves.

At $1,000,000 per Bitcoin, Bitcoin would have a market cap of $21 trillion. Currently the M1 Money Supply, which consists of global checking accounts, coins, and banknotes in circulation, is about $35 trillion. The M2 Money Supply, which includes savings and money market accounts, is around $95.7 trillion. Therefore, it's certainly possible for Bitcoin to reach $100,000 or even $1,000,000 in the future.

10. DO I HAVE TO PAY TAXES ON BITCOIN GAINS?

We'll begin this question by stating that we are not tax professionals, and this is not tax advice. Consult your local professional when filing your tax returns. Make a note that many tax professionals **do not** have experience with cryptocurrency.

But the short answer is yes, you do have to pay taxes on Bitcoin gains.

The IRS (and HMRC in the UK) treats capital gains on cryptocurrency the same way they do stocks. They are considered personal investment assets that you own. Therefore, when you sell your cryptocurrency, you are required to pay capital gains on that amount.

Cryptocurrency is NOT considered gambling (in the UK, gambling wins are exempt from taxation). It also isn't considered a currency for taxation purposes because it is not issued by a central bank.

The IRS states that you must keep a record of your cryptocurrency transactions, including using Bitcoin to pay for goods and services.

The IRS notes the following about BTC and other virtual currencies (*Virtual Currencies*, 2014):

When it comes to Bitcoin, the following are different types of transactions that will lead to taxes:

- Selling Bitcoin, mined personally, to a third party
- Selling Bitcoin, bought from someone (including an exchange), to a third party (including back to the exchange you bought it from)
- Using Bitcoin, which one may have mined, to buy goods or services
- Using Bitcoin, bought from someone, to buy goods or services

The last two points are especially important to note if you plan on using your Bitcoin to pay for goods and services, either online or in person.

WHAT ABOUT SHORT AND LONG-TERM CAPITAL GAINS?

If you hold Bitcoin for less than a year before selling or exchanging, a short-term capital gains tax is applied, which is equal to the ordinary income tax rate for the individual (Kagan, 2019). However, if you hold Bitcoin for more than a year, long-term capital gains tax rates are applied.

It is also important to note that transferring one cryptocurrency for another is considered a transaction and you will have to pay gains on that. However, transferring your Bitcoin from an exchange to a hardware wallet **is not** a taxable event. There has been some confusion regarding this but transferring from one wallet to another is not considered a sale.

To summarize:

Taxable Bitcoin Events	Non-Taxable Bitcoin Events
Selling Bitcoin to a third party	Transferring Bitcoin from an exchange to a wallet
Using Bitcoin to buy goods or services	Transferring Bitcoin from one wallet to another wallet
Trading Bitcoin for another Cryptocurrency on an exchange	Buying Bitcoin with fiat currency
Converting Bitcoin back to Fiat currency on an exchange	

Lastly, do that that you can deduct transaction fees in your tax returns.

FREEMAN BITCOIN INVESTING RULE #4

KEEP TRACK OF ALL YOUR BITCOIN PURCHASES, INCLUDING TIMES YOU CONVERT YOUR BTC BACK TO FIAT

IS MULTIPLE BITCOIN WRITTEN AS "BITCOIN" OR "BITCOINS"?

It's Bitcoin. 1 Bitcoin, 2 Bitcoin, 10,000 Bitcoin. Just like sheep.

4

WHAT AFFECTS BITCOIN PRICES?

W hy does the price of Bitcoin move up and down the way it does? Why is it so volatile? There are no easy answers to these questions. As an asset, BTC is unique. There has never been anything like it before and this makes evaluating it tough.

However, the principles of sound investing have stood the test of time and evaluating BTC from that perspective is helpful. There is almost no fundamental information out there that can affect the price of Bitcoin. We are not talking about macroeconomic factors or government policies that move prices. We are referring to the state of BTC's network and how it's managed.

Because of its decentralized nature, these factors don't change much, if at all. The network cannot be hacked or compromised. The price of BTC as a result has a large speculative portion to it.

In our bestselling book, *The 8-Step Beginner's Guide to Value Investing*, we discussed the 10 principles which determine the long-term price of a company:

- Principle One: The Warren Buffett Test
- Principle Two: Understand the business thoroughly
- Principle Three: Understand the relationship between the Business & the Sector
- Principle Four: If it is a newer company, the founder should still be involved
- Principle Five: Intangible Asset Advantage
- Principle Six: Upper management is bought in
- Principle Seven: The company has strong advertising, marketing & sales operations
- Principle Eight: Management is willing to make short-term sacrifices for long-term results
- Principle Nine: The company has an economic moat
- Principle Ten: The business can weather a storm

Of these 10 principles, only three cannot be applied to Bitcoin: the Buffett test (it is a broader concept that cannot be applied to a currency), the founder principle (BTC doesn't rely on a founder as a company does), and long-term-oriented management (BTC isn't a company with shareholders).

Examining Bitcoin as an asset through the prism of the remaining seven questions will help us understand both its price behavior as well as its qualities as an asset.

UNDERSTAND THE BUSINESS THOROUGHLY

Bitcoin isn't the easiest of investments to understand, but it's far from impossible to do so. We've already covered a lot of information about how it works and why it has inherent value. If you found it tough to grasp these points even after reading them over and over again, we suggest staying away from BTC as an investment. It's best to invest in things you know and understand since you'll be able to take better advantage of tough situations within that asset.

For example, if you wake up one morning and find that the U.S. Government has decided to fully digitize the U.S. Dollar, can you roughly imagine what this might do to the value of BTC? Granted, this is a tough question to answer and one that even economists might struggle to grasp. However, our point is that you don't need to understand just enough to be able to handle a situation.

Most likely, because of its nature, BTC can and will experience massive volatility. Can you hold on to your investment through these ups and downs without giving into the temptation to sell at a seemingly high price and get your money back? Can you avoid listening to the voices in your head that tell you to sell at a low price and be done with the volatility?

Holding onto an investment like BTC is tough because there is so much that is unprecedented. The questions we answered in the previous chapter are just the beginning. They cover the fundamental and technical aspects of BTC. Oftentimes, even things as basic as buying and selling BTC are tough for investors to grasp. This is why it helps to review the information we have provided you and assess whether you're comfortable with it.

How and Where Is BTC Used?

There are still many misperceptions surrounding the use of Bitcoin in the modern economy. Many financial commentators maintain the belief that the majority of Bitcoin transactions are used to perpetrate criminal activity. While this was once the case, it is no longer true. An investigation by the New York Times found that in 2020, just 1% of total Bitcoin transactions were suspected of illegal activity (Popper, 2020). In addition to this, a report by the Society for Worldwide Interbank Financial Telecommunication (SWIFT) stated "[money]-laundering through cryptocurrencies remain relatively small compared to the volumes of cash laundered through traditional methods." While Bitcoin's properties do hold many attractive qualities for criminals, this hardly means there aren't other uses for it.

Bitcoin is increasingly becoming more mainstream than ever with many payment processors now accepting it as a legitimate form of payment. PayPal is the latest company that allows users to transact in Bitcoin. Having said that, the anonymity that BTC provides would be a concern if it were to experience full-scale public adoption. The current financial system exists on norms that are identity driven. Financial intermediaries need to know who is sending money to whom to ascertain whether illegal activity is being carried out. Bitcoin doesn't provide identities and only discloses transaction information. How will Bitcoin mesh with the current order? Or will it overthrow it?

There are no clear answers to this. While crypto evangelists root for an overthrow, it's safe to say that a lot of resources and a number of catalysts are needed for this to happen. Change usually occurs in increments, so expecting Bitcoin to suddenly and dramatically replace a system that has been built over hundreds of years and supports millions of jobs is unrealistic.

It's something an investor in BTC needs to grapple with before they place their money into the asset. Uncertainty is a part of investing in BTC and this is why we counsel investing no more than 10% of your portfolio into it.

INTANGIBLE ASSET ADVANTAGE

Bitcoin gains a lot of momentum and credibility from being the first mover in the cryptocurrency space. As the flag-bearer for a new financial order, it's guaranteed to attract attention, and as time goes on, its pedigree will only grow.

Being the first mover has its advantages and disadvantages. Bitcoin is so popular that in the mind of casual observers it has become synonymous with the blockchain. While this means any news that pushes the advantages of using blockchain over current network capabilities results in free publicity for Bitcoin, in case of negative press, it also affects the reputation of Bitcoin.

Bitcoin has a lot of goodwill baked into it, to use an accounting term. Investing in assets with intangible advantages is great because it means you can rely on it to perform well when times are rough. Perhaps the best example of a company owning an intangible asset advantage is Coca-Cola. It is one of the most recognized brands around the world, and no matter how harsh the times are, you can rest assured that the Coke brand will do well. In fact, thanks to its huge intangible advantage, it'll take a lot of change for any company to replace Coca-Cola or for people around the world to stop drinking it.

The same effect is present in Bitcoin as well. Ask a casual observer about cryptocurrency and the first name they'll drop is Bitcoin. While there are other credible and strong cryptos such as Ethereum, Bitcoin is the one that gains the most exposure. All of this comes despite the other cryptocurrencies possessing certain advantages over Bitcoin.

A scan of the prices of individual coins also reveals the extent of this intangible advantage. For example, one of the knocks against BTC is that it doesn't provide true privacy. Crypto evangelists envisioned a future where all transactions will be fully private and this is what led to the creation of cryptocurrencies like Monero, which is a privacy-focused coin that has been engineered to achieve this from the ground up. Despite this, it is rare to hear about huge moves in Monero, or of institutional investors or crypto evangelists plowing their money into it. All funds seemingly flow towards Bitcoin and this is an advantage that long-term investors can capture.

Every time a global political event happens that threatens stability, the price of Bitcoin automatically rises because the general public thinks that cryptocurrency benefits from instability. Although if you look at the correlation between Bitcoin and the S&P 500 over the past 5 years, you will actually see they are fairly uncorrelated.

Figure 4: The correlation between movement in Bitcoin and the S&P 500 between January 2016 and January 2021 (source: TradingView)

As Bitcoin represents the entire crypto market to many people, it receives the lion's share of price appreciation and funds. Much like how the iPod became synonymous with the term "MP3 player" in the early 2000s, BTC is poised to rake in all the advantages of being a first mover.

We would also like to acknowledge that this can have a negative effect on BTC prices as well since perception can drive prices down more easily. However, in the long run, we believe that the intangible effects that BTC possesses will win and that investors will be rewarded. As greater public adoption continues and as the perception of safety builds, BTC's intangibles will push its prices higher.

UNDERSTAND THE RELATIONSHIP BETWEEN BUSINESS & SECTOR

When evaluating a company, it is critical to check whether it's the business's inherent economics that's driving growth or whether the company is benefiting from a general demand in the sector. For example, you will struggle to find an electric vehicle manufacturer whose stock didn't see a meteoric rise in 2020. However, even a cursory examination of the sector will reveal that there are just one or two companies who have the ability to even produce a working vehicle, let alone turn a profit.

Sector euphoria is something investors don't need to worry about when investing in BTC. This is because BTC **is** the cryptocurrency sector in many ways. At the time of writing BTC makes up close to 68% of all cryptocurrencies in terms of market value. This number is as high as it's been in four years. The current boom in the price of BTC isn't about to subside any time soon either.

If BTC were a company in the cryptocurrency sector, we'd be talking about it as if it were a monopoly. To get a clearer picture of what that means, contrast BTC's position with another company, like Amazon, that's often spoken of as having a monopoly. Everyone would agree that Amazon is a behemoth no matter what their views on the company's practices might be. For the sake of comparison, Amazon's market share of the e-commerce market in the United States is 49% (*10 Fasci-*

nating Amazon Statistics Sellers Need To Know in 2019, 2019). That's 49% of the e-commerce market, not retail. Examine the chatter around Amazon's competitive advantage and how much of a bargain it can strike with its suppliers thanks to its competitive edge and then look at BTC's 68% number. Granted, Bitcoin isn't a company, but that sort of market domination only serves to underline that BTC is what drives cryptocurrency, not the other way around.

BTC is the rising tide that lifts all boats in crypto. In fact, whenever BTC goes through a period of volatility (be it up or down), you can bet that other currencies suffer from it as well. If BTC rises, so does the value of other coins. If it falls, the value of almost every other coin falls. The second largest cryptocurrency, Ethereum, is just 13% of the entire crypto market, small change when compared to BTC. Thus, our belief that BTC is the only cryptocurrency to be owned is reaffirmed.

MOAT

In business terms, a moat is a competitive advantage that allows a business to operate through tough times. A moat can be anything from a patent or a strong brand name to a manufacturing process or the number of users on a network. Economic moats come in all shapes and sizes, and history has proved that companies that have the strongest moats tend to be the ones that survive.

One of the strongest moats to have emerged in recent times is the network effect. The network effect is something that many online businesses enjoy. The greater the number of people that use a product or service, the stronger it becomes. Google is a beneficiary of the network effect. The more people use it to search for information and employ its ancillary services, the more data it gets to collect. The more data it collects, the better it can tailor its services to its users. This in turn ensures that users remain committed to the platform and don't use other search engines or email service providers. Google recognizes the network effect very well and this is why it gives away all of its services for free. Technically speaking, it doesn't charge users money, but users pay with data.

Facebook is another business that makes a living using the network effect. It does everything it can to keep users on its platform and makes no bones about wanting data. This data is used to personalize a user's experience and keep them coming back for more.

How does BTC stand with regards to the network effect? Turns out that it has benefitted massively from it too. As we discussed in chapter 2, one of the biggest hurdles to Bitcoin's growth has been mass acceptance. If most people around the globe won't use it, then it is of no value to anyone. Much like any form of money, if no one is willing to accept that BTC is an acceptable legal tender, then it ceases to have any value.

Over the previous decade, BTC has steadily gained public trust and is an acceptable form of payment at various venues. Microsoft, AT&T, Virgin Galactic, Namecheap, and Norwegian Air are just a few businesses that accept Bitcoin payments. In the sports world, the Dallas Mavericks, Miami Dolphins, and Portuguese soccer club Benfica are a few examples of teams that also accept BTC payments. Politically, Miami Mayor Francis Suarez announced an initiative which allowed city workers to receive their salary in Bitcoin.

Paypal made a splash recently when it announced that it would accept and process BTC payments. Empire Flippers, a company that facilitates the buying and selling of online businesses, also facilitates BTC payments. In the fast-food world, Burger King in Venezuela and KFC in Canada accept payments in BTC. Additionally, a 2020 survey found that 36% of small and midsize businesses in the United States now accept Bitcoin.

These aren't small numbers. Add to this the seal of approval that most institutional financial managers have given BTC and you have a recipe for mass adoption. As BTCs adoption increases, it stands to reason that its value will increase. The more people transact BTC and mine it, the more scarce and therefore valuable it becomes. All of this is a classic example of how the network effect preserves a company's competitive edge. Look at the example of Facebook. The company has faced a number of legal battles and isn't a company that people trust very much. However, the platform is still popular and continues to be so due to the sheer number of users that inhabit it.

STRONG SALES AND MARKETING

Sales and marketing are business functions that you wouldn't associate with a cryptocurrency. After all, it isn't as if BTC is a company with a staff that can market it to consumers. However, BTC is unique in that it has the first mover advantage. This means it has the backing of powerful influencers in the technology and financial space, and this lends it a lot of credibility.

While the movie *The Social Network* initially portrayed them as the people who lost out to Mark Zuckerberg and Facebook, the Winklevoss twins have turned out to be absolutely correct about Bitcoin's rise. They were amongst the first to preach the gospel of cryptocurrency and both brothers are now worth $1 billion each. The twins aren't alone in cheering for Bitcoin.

Andreas Antonopoulos is another Bitcoin evangelist who regularly talks about the benefits of the cryptocurrency. Antonopoulos's background in founding tech companies gives him a unique insight into how the technology works as well as how it could shape up in the future. Acclaimed personal finance author Robert Kiyosaki is also a huge fan of BTC, having proclaimed recently that $50,000 is a reasonable value for BTC. This is quite an about-face for him since he's a noted advocate of investing in precious metals such as silver and platinum.

He may not be an evangelist, but Paul Tudor Jones is one of the most famous traders to ever grace the financial markets, and naturally made waves recently when he announced that he'll be buying BTC for his clients' portfolios as a hedge against the dollar. Other notable investors piling into BTC include Stan Druckenmiller and Michael Novogratz, a former hedge fund manager and Goldman Sachs executive.

The narrative around Bitcoin also serves as a very effective marketing strategy. While the initial chatter about overhauling the world's financial system has settled down, there's no denying that BTC addresses many flaws in the current system. These flaws are something every person can relate to, whether you're a billionaire or an everyday Joe/Jane on the street. BTC's narrative holds appeal and promise for every class of investor, and the backing of these famous people only serves to fuel its legitimacy and its value continues to soar. When it comes to strong marketing, BTC has an abundance of firepower.

INSIDER BUYING

A key component of a good investment purchase is strong and heavy insider buying. Executives buying shares of their companies indicates that better times lie ahead and it's about as strong a vote of confidence as any company can receive. BTC isn't a company, so how can we evaluate it?

It might not be a company, but it does have a founder. Satoshi Nakamoto still holds "his" original 1.1 million BTC. This information is public because the wallet addresses associated with this entity can be reverse-engineered and monitored. Since Nakamoto's holdings correspond to the very first node established on the BTC network, their transactions can be monitored. While they might have other wallets, the bulk of their holdings reside in the first node.

BTC owners can monitor their networks in real time for any transactions originating from Nakamoto's wallet. Hence, there's very strong evidence of insider holdings, far more than what any SEC filing can provide.

IT CAN WEATHER A STORM

The true test of any asset is how well it weathers bad times. Any asset can do well in a bull market. As the saying goes, "a rising tide lifts all boats." However, bad times are the real test for whether a company's management has been running things properly or whether an asset is truly built to withstand tough times.

And how does BTC fare in this regard? Well, for the majority of its existence BTC has been exposed to bad times. It was born amidst one of the worst crises to hit the world with storm-weathering qualities built right into it. It operates on a network that cannot be hacked, is guaranteed a limited supply, and has a founder who is fully invested in it.

BTC has a number of influencers who believe in it and continue to push it forward as an alternative source of money. To put it simply, BTC is anti-fragile. Any disruption or disturbance that occurs in the global economy benefits BTC. It doesn't just weather storms, it thrives in them. Its anti-fragility is so stark that its price tends to dip during good times.

This explains the volatility that the currency experiences. BTC trading is marked by massive price rises and equally massive falls.

However, despite every fall and doubts that have been thrown its way, it keeps bouncing back up and refuses to go away. The only question to ask is, is there anything within BTC's inherent architecture that might trip an investor up?

Given that it exists on the blockchain, where counterfeiting and forced theft are impossible, it's hard to see flaws that could cause the system to crash. This isn't to say that BTC doesn't have any flaws. But, there are no major flaws that could result in your investment being wiped out completely.

Bitcoin is more than just a currency. It is a hybrid of an asset and a currency. Imagine if the EUR/USD currency exchange pair behaved like real estate does. That's how BTC behaves and that's what makes it complex yet reliable.

FREEMAN BITCOIN INVESTING RULE #5

EVEN THOUGH BITCOIN IS A CURRENCY, YOU CAN STILL EVALUATE IT USING SOUND INVESTING PRINCIPLES

OTHER BTC PRICE DRIVERS

Aside from the fundamentals we've just discussed, there are other drivers of BTC prices. Most of them originate from the macro-economic conditions around the world. These factors can be tough to analyze individually, though there are some clear global patterns that have established themselves over the course of the previous decade.

FREEMAN PUBLICATIONS

Fiat Currency Inflation

We've already covered the negative effects quantitative easing measures have had on the value of paper money. The rate at which money is being printed has only increased over time. As the COVID-19 pandemic hit the world, governments began printing even more money. In 2020, the U.S. Fed printed $3.38 trillion dollars in the form of economic stimulus. This means one in five dollars in circulation currently has been freshly printed.

Printing money now is a lot like borrowing money from the future to pay bills now. It isn't free and comes at the cost of inflation. While it's impossible to predict the exact rate at which inflation will increase, there's no doubt that the value of cash will depreciate faster than it has ever in history.

This is why finding a stable hedge for a declining dollar is so important. It is also why institutional investors have pushed money into gold and BTC as a means of preserving wealth. The exodus from cash is sure to push the price of BTC and other cryptocurrency higher and this makes it an extremely attractive investment.

Less Regulation

When BTC first burst onto the scene, governments reacted as they always do to something revolutionary and banned it. It was branded as being suitable only for frauds and criminals. Fast forward to today and governments around the globe have begun loosening regulations around cryptocurrencies. In the United States, the government has opened the financial system up to so-called stablecoins.

These coins are connected to readily identifiable assets such as gold or to recognizable commodities such as the U.S. Dollar. They formalized the introduction of blockchain as a means of financial transfer, making blockchain as acceptable a form of data transfer as ACH or

SWIFT. Anyone who has ever used the latter networks will appreciate the efficiency with which the blockchain works.

The changing attitude toward BTC amongst the financial elite is perhaps explained by them finally waking up to the current inefficiencies within the system they created. Cryptocurrencies are now a part and parcel of the American financial system, and other countries are sure to follow.

Institutional Adoption

We touched on institutional adoption previously, but it's hard to undersell the impact that institutional money managers have had on legitimizing BTC and on pushing its price to new highs. Paul Tudor Jones and Stan Druckenmiller are two of the most high-profile money managers to move money into Bitcoin.

Here are their views:

The best profit-maximizing strategy is to own the fastest horse ... If I am forced to forecast, my bet is it will be Bitcoin.

— PAUL TUDOR JONES

Bitcoin could be an asset class that has a lot of attraction as a store of value to both millennials and the new West Coast money and, as you know, they got a lot of it

— STAN DRUCKENMILLER

It isn't just hedge fund managers who have been pouring money into BTC. Insurance companies have also begun directing their portfolios towards cryptocurrencies. Massachusetts Mutual Life Insurance recently announced a purchase of $100 million worth of BTC.

All this institutional demand is only driving BTC prices higher than ever before. While long-term investors shouldn't be concerned about speculative price bubbles, there is no doubt that institutional adoption paves the way for greater mainstream exposure.

Mainstream Adoption

As more and more institutions begin investing in BTC, it is only a matter of time before payment processors and vendors start offering it to their customers. PayPal is an example of a processor that has already started allowing its customers to buy, sell, or hold BTC. Moves such as these will only lead to greater mass adoption of the cryptocurrency.

While Bitcoin is still a long way away from being accepted on the same plane as the U.S Dollar, remember that we're still very early in the Bitcoin story. There is a long way to go yet and the signs of mass adoption at this point are extremely encouraging. There are signs of massive retail demand for BTC, as evidenced by the image on the following page.

Figure 5: Trends Search of Bitcoin Price Versus Tesla Price (source: Google Trends)

While Google Trends isn't an indicator of where future prices will go, it does accurately reflect what people around the world are thinking about. Tesla has been one of the darlings of the stock market in recent years and its CEO does his bit to keep publicizing his company. Tesla also belongs to a hot sector, electric vehicles, and there is no doubt that it is on everyone's mind.

As the number of searches for Tesla's stock price has grown, the stock has rocketed upwards, split, and has increased some more. The demand is so high that Tesla is planning on raising even more money from the stock market. There's seemingly no end to the bull run in that stock.

If Tesla can generate such high returns for its investors, then extrapolating the Google Trends graph for BTC implies explosive growth. BTC is nowhere near as accessible as Tesla is and this is why its price hasn't exploded as much. However, it has embarked on a bull run that dwarfs Tesla's nonetheless. All of this goes to show the effects of retail demand on asset prices and how BTC is poised to increase in value massively.

5

HOW TO BUY BITCOIN IN FIVE MINUTES

There was a time when you needed to possess serious software and technical chops to buy BTC and other cryptocurrencies. These days, buying cryptos is no more complex than buying regular stocks – in just a few clicks. There are a number of support services that allow you to buy and sell cryptocurrencies no matter where you are in the world. In this chapter, we're going to briefly walk you through the processes of buying and selling BTC.

COINBASE

The most beginner-friendly option is Coinbase and it is the one we recommend. Coinbase is a crypto brokerage that allows you to buy and sell as many cryptocurrencies as you want.

The crypto market is open 24/7/365 unlike stocks. Stocks trade on an exchange that has opening and closing hours, but cryptocurrencies trade on worldwide networks instead of exchanges. This means the market is always open.

Once you buy Bitcoin on Coinbase, you should transfer it to your hardware wallet immediately instead of holding it on the exchange. Because of Bitcoin's volatility, we also recommend setting up recurring purchases on Coinbase since this is a great way to automate your investment and ignore short term market moves.

In fact, over the past 5 years, buying Bitcoin every week performed better than timing the market 82% of the time.

SETTING UP AUTOMATED RECURRING BUYS

If you want a "set it and forget it" approach which uses dollar cost averaging to buy BTC, here is how to set it up on your Coinbase app.

Step 1: To use this option you must link a bank account to Coinbase, the same way you would with your regular brokerage if you wanted to make automated purchases. We always recommend using direct bank accounts purchases because you will pay just 1% vs. 4% if you use a debit card.

On the mobile app, the link is at the bottom right of the home screen under "settings"

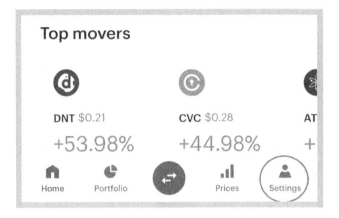

Step 2: How to set up automated purchases on the mobile app:

3. Choose Bitcoin from the "Select Asset to Buy" Screen

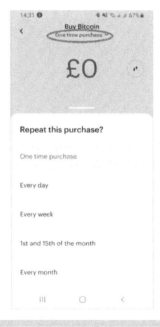

✕	Select asset to buy	
Bitcoin BTC		$40,472.99 +5.75%
Ethereum ETH		$1,696.67 −1.15%
Litecoin LTC		$161.29 +3.50%
Chainlink LINK		$25.59 −2.52%
Bitcoin Cash BCH		$482.53 +8.68%

4. Tap on "On-Time Purchase" to bring up the recurring purchase screen and choose your desired purchase frequency.

14:31

Buy Bitcoin
One time purchase

£0

Repeat this purchase?

One time purchase

Every day

Every week

1st and 15th of the month

Every month

We've also recorded a full video tutorial for setting up recurring purchases in Coinbase. You can find that, as well as the rest of our Bitcoin 101 videos at

https://freemanpublications.com/bonus

FREEMAN BITCOIN INVESTING RULE #6

TO MAKE PRICE FLUCTUATIONS LESS OF AN ISSUE, USE DOLLAR COST AVERAGING WHEN BUYING BITCOIN

6

THREE WAYS TO NOT BUY BITCOIN

There are other ways in which you can buy Bitcoin, but almost all of them have significant drawbacks. In this chapter, we're going to illustrate three of these ways and why you should stay away from them at all costs.

ROBINHOOD

Robinhood is one of the most popular apps to trade stocks with. Because of its "zero cost investing" disruption card, it has managed to attract a large number of users. Robinhood offers its users the opportunity to buy BTC. However, there are many caveats you should be aware of.

First, you don't own the Bitcoin you buy. Robinhood buys it for you and stores it in their own online wallets. You don't have access to it as a result and cannot prove ownership of your BTC. Thus, you cannot withdraw it to your hardware wallet and must exchange it for fiat currency before you withdraw your holdings.

Robinhood positions itself as a zero-fee broker, but this isn't the case with cryptocurrencies. You will be charged a hefty commission, which will significantly reduce your holdings. Overall, buying BTC on Robinhood is like buying a computer via Amazon, except instead of sending you the computer, Amazon sends you a picture of it in your warehouse with your name scrawled on it to prove ownership.

It's a bad deal that you should stay away from at all costs.

GBTC

Grayscale Bitcoin Trust or GBTC is a popular BTC buying option. It works like an ETF -the fund manager buys BTC using the money you give them. Note that crypto ETFs are still not permitted to operate, which is why this instrument is legally a trust and trades like a regular stock does.

You can own GBTC in your IRA or 401(k) and you might think this makes it a perfect way to dip your toes in BTC. Since it's a traditional investment vehicle, you won't need any fancy wallets or private keys to pass it on to your heirs. It fits well with the currency way in which most investors operate. However, dig a little deeper and you'll see that GBTC isn't a great option. For starters, the trust trades at a premium to BTC prices. BTC is driven by speculative demand quite a lot over the short term, so you're guaranteed to be paying a little too much for your holdings. Additionally, you don't actually own any Bitcoin; you'll own shares in the trust, which isn't the same thing.

The biggest drawback is the management fee. GBTC charges a two percent annual management fee, based on the value of your investment. This means you will be paying two percent no matter what. This is a significant hurdle to overcome, even before you take the premium into account. Over the past year, GBTC's premium has fluctuated between five to 20%. Imagine buying an asset that needs to earn 27% before breaking even!

That's why GBTC is a poor deal for long-term investors.

BITW

The Bitwise 10 Crypto Index Fund or BITW is an index fund that tracks a basket of cryptocurrencies. BITW promises to give you access to the entire crypto market through a simple investment, much like SPY does with the S&P 500 index. But does it live up to its promises? Figure 6 is a good place to begin this evaluation.

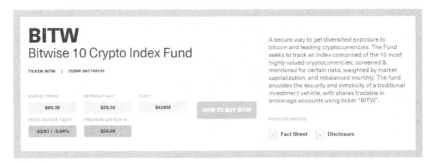

Figure 6: BITW Specifics

BITW holds 84% Bitcoin, 11% Ethereum, and the rest is divided between other currencies. As far as representing the crypto market goes, this is a fair distribution. However, there are other issues that prevent it from being a good investment. For starters, the fund charges a 2.5% expense fee, which is extremely high. In comparison, SPY charges 0.09%.

Figure 6, captured in January 2021, also illustrates the biggest problem with BITW. The fund has a NAV of $28.36 and a price of $60.39, adding up to a premium of 113%. There is no way an investor will be able to overcome that hurdle in a short time. If the price of BTC drops, your losses will be exaggerated since the premium will fall along with the asset's price. Besides, would you ever pay 113% extra for anything, be it stocks or gold?

The other issue is that the fund trades only on weekdays while the crypto market is open throughout the week. This means any moves over the weekend could leave you defenseless and you could lose a lot of money. Buying BTC directly is a far better option.

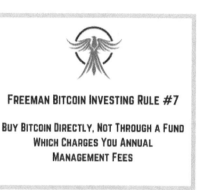

FREEMAN BITCOIN INVESTING RULE #7

BUY BITCOIN DIRECTLY, NOT THROUGH A FUND WHICH CHARGES YOU ANNUAL MANAGEMENT FEES

7

KEEPING YOUR BITCOIN SAFE

Bitcoin's history is punctuated with events when investors lost their coins due to committing basic storage errors. The electronic nature of this asset makes people think their crypto assets are vulnerable to hacking. This is true to an extent, but it is based on a major misconception. In reality, it's often human error that results in major losses.

Learning how to store your Bitcoin is an important part of being an intelligent investor. Most investors who have operated in the stock market have never had to deal with considering storage since the existing financial system takes care of it for you. However, when it comes to cryptocurrency it's a bad idea to leave your coins with an exchange or in another entity's wallet. This makes you vulnerable to being hacked. Besides, if you store your coins with someone else, there is no way you can prove you are the owner.

You might think that buying BTC and storing it in a service's wallet is a lot like storing your money in a bank. However, this isn't the case. Banks have been around for centuries now and follow strict regulatory guidelines. Crypto storage services don't have anywhere near that kind of scrutiny on them just yet. This is why you must always store your coins on your own infrastructure.

The word infrastructure makes it seem as if you need to own server farms, but this isn't the case. All you need is a crypto wallet that can store your keys. Remember that a key is your password and is tied to the wallet address on the blockchain network.

WALLETS

There are different kinds of cryptocurrency wallets you can use to store your BTC. Your wallet is your crypto bank account and stores vital information regarding your holdings. Note that your wallet doesn't store your coins. Your coins are present on the blockchain and can never be replicated or stolen. Your wallet stores information that gives you access to your coins. This means if you lose your physical wallet; you can still recover your cryptocurrency. Your wallet is the gatekeeper to the blockchain, and you should always store it safely.

All Bitcoin wallets have two keys, or passwords, that the wallet holds. The first is a public key and the second is a private key. The public key is the address at which your Bitcoin is held. The private key is a randomly generated string that functions as a transaction password. If you wish to send or receive BTC, you need to validate that transaction using your private key. Let's say someone wants to send you BTC. You provide them your public key and enter your private key on the wallet software. This validates the transaction on the network and your coins increase (or decrease if you're sending payment to someone).

There are different types of wallets. Let's look at which ones are the best for you.

Desktop Wallet

A desktop wallet is a software program that rests on your PC. To transact in BTC, you'll need to log into your desktop to validate your transactions. Desktop wallets are safer compared to some of the other options on this list, but they aren't ideal. The biggest hurdle is that you cannot make transactions on the fly or on the move. This makes them potentially cumbersome. The other issue with desktop wallets is that if your desktop is compromised, you might end up losing your coins. If you don't update your desktop OS with the latest antivirus and malware protection, you are going to be running massive risks.

Mobile Wallets

A mobile wallet exists as an app on your smartphone. While transacting BTC through a mobile app is easier, you're open to even bigger risks in terms of having your phone hacked or compromised in some way. There is also the fact that many mobile wallets don't store information locally; they store it on a network or server elsewhere. This essentially makes mobile wallet software a front for the next option we are going to discuss.

Online Wallet

An online wallet is a service provided by a third-party provider. You can sign up for their service and task them with storing your keys. If you open an account with Coinbase or any other service that allows you to transact in BTC, you are using an online wallet. The Mt. Gox incident is a cautionary tale of how online wallets can be compromised. Mt. Gox's security measures were weak, to say the least, and this resulted in massive theft.

You're dependent on the online service to keep upgrading their security and investing in it constantly. We don't recommend using online wallets since you are not in control of your keys.

Hardware Wallets

Hardware Wallets are the most secure way to store your keys. A hardware wallet is a USB device that stores your keys. It isn't connected to the internet until you plug it in, making it close to impossible to hack. If the device were ever stolen from your person, no one can log into it or steal your keys since it often comes with high-tech security features. However, losing your hardware wallet and your private key will result in your losing your holdings, so be careful.

Any damage to the wallet or compromise to its structure might result in it malfunctioning. You could lose access to your funds if you lose your private key. You need to be as careful as possible and follow the best practices that we will outline shortly. Two popular hardware wallets are the Ledger Nano series and the Trezor wallets. These will cost you around $70.

Our personal preference is the Ledger Nano Wallet and we have a video tutorial showing you how to set yours up in the Bitcoin 101 bonus section of this book, which you can find at

http://freemanpublications.com/bonus

FREEMAN BITCOIN INVESTING RULE #8

FOR MAXIMUM SECURITY, ALWAYS STORE
YOUR BITCOIN OFFLINE.

Paper Wallets

Paper wallets might sound incongruous, but they're impossible to hack because they're literally pieces of paper with your keys printed on them in the form of QR codes. While they're safe electronically, they carry high risks physically. A piece of paper can be torn or lost or misplaced, resulting in loss of access to funds. We have found that it is best to stick with a hardware wallet that is far sturdier.

Wallet Best Practices

Always purchase wallets from trusted sources. You can buy the two wallets we recommended from their websites or from trusted third-party sellers like Amazon. Do not buy wallets from unknown third-party sellers or from websites like eBay. This isn't to say eBay is bad. It's just that you can never verify your seller completely.

Do not buy used hardware wallets since you can never know if the software within it is programmed to steal your keys. Guard your keys and never share it anywhere publicly. Remember your public key can be seen on the network but no one can conduct transactions without your private key. Therefore, guard it with your heart at all times.

Since a BTC address can link to all of your past transactions and your crypto balance, it is important you make use of different addresses to receive payments if you are dealing with large amounts of cryptocurrency. In the same way you can have multiple bank accounts, you can own multiple wallets to store your BTC separately. Once you start making use of different addresses, no one will be able to trace all these transactions back to you. People who send you Bitcoin cannot see how many coins you own or your past transactions.

Finally, never brag about owning a large amount of BTC. Much like bragging about money or gold, this makes you a target. All it takes is one malicious actor to compromise your holdings. These days phishing is a common tactic that malicious actors use to steal information. Figure 5 illustrates a common tactic these days where real websites are spoofed.

Note the domain name in Figure 7: instead of "ledger.com", it reads "le**gd**er.com." Always follow some common-sense security tactics and you and your BTC will be fine.

Figure 7: A Fake Website Posing as a Legitimate Online Wallet

Be wary of links and be cautious when asked to install software. If you receive emails that ask you to do this, take note of the email addresses and ask someone else to verify whether the email looks genuine. Carefully review all suspicious emails or texts you receive over the phone.

Never type your private key recovery words into anything online. Maintain your web browser and keep it updated with the latest patches. Be mindful of surprises, tune out of the sense of urgency, and watch out for the hook. Attackers prey on a sense of urgency, and you can avoid many attacks by simply waiting for a few days.

8

AVOIDING BTC SCAMS

Whenever something new pops onto the scene, you can almost always expect Ponzi schemes to accompany it. With Bitcoin and its talk of revolutionizing the financial system, it was just a matter of time before con artists began using it to commit fraud against the public. Unfortunately, many of these frauds taint Bitcoin's reputation and scare people away.

However, you have nothing to fear if you follow the tips and pointers we've outlined thus far. Nonetheless, it would be negligent of us to neglect to inform you of the different types of scams you might encounter. One of the most common scams is the Initial Coin Offering of an alternative cryptocurrency or altcoin. Let's take a look at that first.

THE ICO SCAM

Before we dive in, we'd like to point out that not all ICOs are fraudulent. Similar to an IPO in the stock investing world, an ICO is simply an event where a coin is issued to investors for the first time. Whether that coin has any value or not is debatable and this is where fraud enters the picture. There have been numerous examples of scam artists launching altcoins "like Bitcoin" that have lured investors to give them money.

Some of these scams have bordered on ridiculous, but they show how vulnerable people are when it comes to money. One infamous example involved a man named Aziz Mirza who launched the "Bitcoin of the Middle East," termed "habibi coin." Apparently, the name wasn't enough to alert investors to the fraud. Mirza raised over five million dollars and managed to lose it all when he finally got arrested (*Canadian in Dubai Arrested for Fraud, Including Crypto Fraud via Habibi Coin, the "Bitcoin of the Middle East,"* 2019).

Another popular scam was perpetrated by Ruja Ignatova, or "Dr. Ruja," as she was called by the members of her Onecoin scam. Ignatova and her brother Konstantin Ignatov managed to lure investors by cooking up conspiracy theories and got them to invest with them. Once the game was up, Ignatova disappeared and this led to a round of theories about how "powerful financial forces" had kidnapped her since Onecoin was on the verge of revolutionizing the system (Bartlett, 2019).

While these tales are exceptional, they show that scam artists will use Bitcoin and its promise to try to steal your money. Be wary of anyone offering you altcoins or "Bitcoin-like" offerings. There are many legitimate ICOs, but all of them try to improve the existing cryptocurrency framework by introducing features that BTC and existing currencies lack.

Therefore, the very mention of a new cryptocurrency that is "like Bitcoin" should be a signal that something is off. If you're still interested in investing, make sure you read the whitepaper - a technical document that outlines the purpose of the currency and what it aims to achieve - that backs the currency. Most fraudulent currencies won't have a whitepaper. Even if they do, you'll find them amateurishly written with a ton of mistakes and language that makes no sense.

MONEY-MAKING SCHEMES

While offering altcoins is a popular trap laid by scam artists, another trick these people use is to offer you an investing program of some kind where you can receive your money back within a ludicrously short period of time. You might be approached by a bunch of crypto experts who will claim to have earned returns of over a thousand percent over a period of a few years thanks to a "super-secret trading system".

We must note that the crypto market has increased by more than 1000% over the past decade or so. However, it doesn't take a genius to make money in the crypto market. All one has to do is buy and hold. In a bull market, every bullish strategy works, so it's not as if these people have developed a system that no one else has discovered. As we mentioned earlier, a rising tide lifts all boats.

If you do wish to invest with someone, look for a person who has been doing this for a long time and knows what they are talking about. When evaluating their performance, make sure to ask questions about how scalable their system is. If it works in the crypto markets, it ought to work in other markets as well. While there are exceptions, if you hear anything about the "unique nature of the crypto market," then you should instantly know that the strategy isn't anything special a buy and hold strategy cannot replicate.

LENDING SCHEMES

These have been the worst schemes that have been used to rob the public. Most of them have made no sense and have only appealed to those who are greedy. The way these schemes work is similar to money-making schemes. It involves investors putting money into the coin and then receiving periodic payouts from the organizers. It seems astonishing, but no one seems to ask where the money will actually come from.

The most high-profile case thus far was that of Bitconnect. A cryptocurrency lending program that marketed itself as offering 40% monthly returns to users. They guaranteed that at this interest rate, an initial $1,000 investment would be worth more than $50 million within 3 years.

The founders claimed this was possible and sustainable due to the use of a Bitcoin trading bot, and for a short period of time, many naïve investors believed their claims. In fact, at one point at the end of 2017, Bitconnect was in the top 20 most successful cryptocurrency tokens. However, a cease and desist order in January of 2018 forced the founders behind the scheme to shut it down, with investors losing millions.

Many other copycat operations have popped up since then. Here are some of the most noteworthy scams that have adhered to this format:

- Davorcoin
- Falconcoin
- PlusCoin
- OneToken

AUTOMATED TRADING SYSTEMS

Automation is all the rage these days, but when it comes to cryptocurrencies or anything to do with making money, run for the hills. Like in the Forex trading world, there are many scam artists selling so-called "automated trading systems" that promise you absurd returns. Remember that if anyone had a true automated system which could generate profits on autopilot, they would have no need to ever sell it.

As we mentioned previously, it's been relatively easy to make money in Bitcoin over the past decade with a simple buy and hold strategy. Therefore, if you've never traded stocks or regular financial instruments previously, we recommend staying away from trading cryptocurrencies.

FREEMAN BITCOIN INVESTING RULE #9

IF IT SOUNDS TOO GOOD TO BE TRUE, IT PROBABLY IS

9

HOW TO PROFIT FROM THE BITCOIN BOOM IN THE STOCK MARKET

While directly buying Bitcoin is the best move for you if you wish to add it to your portfolio, there are other ways to gain exposure to it. One of the best ways is to buy stocks of companies that have significant exposure to BTC. In this chapter, we're going to focus on companies whose fortunes are either directly tied to BTC's or who will stand to benefit from its wider adoption.

COMPANIES ENABLING BITCOIN ADOPTION

The first category of companies we'll look at are established entities that have profitable businesses or businesses that are on stable ground. Adding BTC to their stable of offerings only strengthens them, and as the price of Bitcoin rises, you can expect these companies to gain ground as well.

PayPal

We first recommended PayPal in our book *The 8-Step Beginner's Guide to Value Investing* and the stock is up 50% since then. PayPal is a behemoth in the payment providers space and doesn't have any significant competition. It's the go-to service for merchants and online workers who wish to get paid. While it doesn't have a complete monopoly, it does have a very strong economic moat that ensures its business will survive tough times.

In October 2020, PayPal announced it would allow cryptocurrency transactions on its platform and would also process crypto payments to merchants on its platform. Currently, the company has 325 million users and 26 million merchants. PayPal has been enabling other ways of withdrawing cryptocurrency before this announcement. It has a good relationship with Coinbase that stretches back to 2016 and has allowed Coinbase users to transfer their fiat money to PayPal since 2018.

PayPal also owns Venmo and cryptocurrency transactions will be enabled on the latter in 2021. Venmo has recently enabled payments to merchants and this will increase the frequency of cryptocurrency transactions on the platform. Investing in PayPal is much more than just about Bitcoin. However, as Bitcoin stands to be adopted by the masses, there's no doubt PayPal will benefit from it and will also enable greater adoption at the same time.

Coinbase

We must point out that Coinbase isn't a public company yet and that retail investors cannot purchase shares in it. However, Coinbase has recently submitted a Form S-1, which is a strong signal of their intent to file an IPO. As of their last funding round, Coinbase had a valuation of eight billion dollars. This was in 2018.

Since then, the demand for its services has increased and along with the value of BTC. As the largest enabler of cryptocurrency trading in the world, there's no doubt that Coinbase stands to gain from the surge of interest that retail investors have in cryptos.

Our conservative estimate places Coinbase's valuation at at least double its previous valuation. With crypto interest only continuing to grow, there's no doubt that Coinbase will be a massive IPO play once it debuts on the markets.

Bitmain

Bitmain was founded in 2013, back before BTC or cryptocurrency was considered mainstream as it is today. The company's mission was quite simple. They built (and continue to build) machines that help people mine Bitcoin and cryptocurrencies. Bitmain is headquartered in Beijing, China, and was valued at over $1 billion in 2017, which was its last funding round.

By 2018, the company became the world's largest manufacturer of ASIC chips that are used to mine BTC. The company also opened other lines of business by running two of the largest BTC mining pools in the world, namely BTC.com and Antpool. However, do note that Bitmain has had its share of controversies, having already been embroiled in high-profile court cases where it was alleged that the company was mining coins on its devices using customer electricity.

Regardless, the company is already profitable and is projected to continue showing profitability going forward. It first planned an IPO in 2018 to be listed on the Hong Kong stock exchange. However, a crash in Bitcoin prices deterred the board from going ahead with their plans. The company is set to proceed with an IPO in mid-2021 in Hong Kong.

This means Robinhood traders won't be able to purchase any stock but more sophisticated brokerage platforms will be able to give you access to it. The company is expected to raise over $18 billion in its IPO and will become the largest pure play on cryptocurrency in the markets. With regards to the various "crypto mining" companies listed on the stock market, we are most bullish on Bitmain and you should be too.

Canaan Inc.

Canaan happens to be the very first company we recommended to our readers back in March 2020. Like Bitmain, this small-cap Chinese company manufactures mining equipment for its customers. Unlike Bitmain, it doesn't have the same degree of backing, and has struggled a bit during its tenure.

Between June 2019 and June 2020, Canaan's revenues fell by 47% and the company posted a net loss of $12.3 million by Q3 2020. Its PS ratio is currently 101, which can make it seem like an absurd investment. However, Canaan's fortunes are directly tied to Bitcoin's price. The company was projected to be profitable only if BTC was above $15,000. Currently, BTC is trading at twice that number.

Despite this, Canaan is a speculative play and is a risky investment. However, given the boost we expect all crypto mining manufacturers to receive, this company seems set to cash in on the overall sector interest.

COMPANIES THAT PIVOTED

The boom in Bitcoin has led to some truly strange stories and investment opportunities. The companies we are going to feature next can either be viewed as incompetent or as visionaries. Regardless of the wider perception, we believe they stand to gain immensely from the surge of interest in BTC and cryptocurrency because they have decided to tie their fortunes directly to it.

Riot Blockchain

We have to start any discussion about Riot Blockchain by mentioning that this company's stock surged by 1,500% in 2020 with the increase in BTC's price. And that's not all, the company's story itself is quite strange. Back in 2017, this company was a biotech startup with just six employees. At some point, the founders saw the writing on the wall and decided to pivot to mining cryptocurrencies.

In December 2019, the company bought 15,000 Antminer S19 Bitcoin mining rigs from Bitmain back in 2019 when the cost of mining cryptocurrency was greater than the value of the coins themselves. This marked a capacity increase of 33% for them. The company kept mining coins and is now profiting from a surge in the value of BTC. However, dealing with energy costs is still a challenge for them. Practically, no one on Wall Street knows what to make of this company. However, if you are on the lookout for a company that hoards a large amount of BTC, Riot Blockchain is it.

MicroStrategy

As far as company names go, MicroStrategy is probably not an accurate description of what this company does. There's nothing micro about it, and the management doesn't seem to have much of a strategy either. This company produces business intelligence software and cloud-based services for its clients. It was founded back in 1989 when its founder landed a consulting contract with DuPont and $250,000 as seed capital.

MicroStrategy went from strength to strength as it brought rigid analytical framework to its clients' sales data and enabled them to make better business decisions. At one point in the mid-90s, the company included McDonald's in one of its many clients. The 90s was a successful decade for them and they decided to go public at the turn of the millennium.

The company began to go pear-shaped soon after. It kept releasing products that were well received by the market, but the lack of quality started drawing attention. The company started erroneously exaggerating its accounting results, as more clients left the company. An SEC fine followed, and layoffs began.

A decade later, it didn't seem like MicroStrategy had much of a future. As a last Hail Mary, the company pivoted to creating business intelligence tools and providing cloud software analytics platforms to its clients, hoping to gain from the boom in big data. This hasn't panned out very well either since the company lacks the technical know-how to compete with other intelligence tools providers like Sisense or IBM.

Are you wondering why we have we included this company on this list? Well, it happens to hold an insane amount of BTC. In August 2020, the company announced it was moving $250 million of reserve cash into BTC. This amount increased over the following months and as of December 1, 2020, the company held 70,470 BTC, valued at over $1 billion. By the end of January 2021, they had reached $2.2 Billion. Microstrategy's BTC position now dwarfs the rest of their business by a large amount.

Figure 8*: Comparing the performance of MicroStrategy stock vs. Bitcoin (source: TradingView)*

This interest in BTC, combined with an increase in its price saw Microstrategy's stock price surge by almost 400% in the past 12 months, roughly in line with the increase in BTC prices. However, there is some confusion regarding the company's strategy because unlike Riot Blockchain, MicroStrategy is not a miner. The company simply bought BTC with its cash on hand. In fact, they even borrowed money to buy coins, and they do not plan on using them in any way to augment the current business. The company also does not have any plans to pivot to the cryptocurrency sector. This is probably a good thing though, given the company's track record.

By all accounts, MicroStrategy was a company going nowhere. However, today it happens to be sitting on a goldmine. Its price is divorced from its core business and if you want a speculative play on the price of BTC without actually buying any coins, MicroStrategy is a good bet.

The Best Blockchain ETF

Whenever a growth industry like blockchain emerges, a number of investment banks and market makers will launch their own ETFs to capitalize on the interest in the sector. Blockchain is no different, and in the past 12 months alone a number of new ETFs have been launched.

Many of these are thinly traded, and thus are subject to manipulation. Therefore, when it comes to buying an ETF, the two most important metrics are volume and assets under management. With both of these metrics, the larger, the better strategy always works.

At present, the most well rounded blockchain ETF is the **Siren Nasdaq NexGen Economy ETF** which trades under the ticker symbol BLCN. Compared to its competitors, it has a lower expense ratio (0.68%) and a well-diversified holding of 70 companies. Owning BLCN gives you exposure to crypto mining manufacturers like Canaan Inc (the second largest holding), as well as financial companies set to benefit from the BTC boom like Square and Signature Bank.There are other blockchain ETFs on the market like KOIN and BLOK, but BLCN remains our preferred one.

10

WILL BITCOIN CRASH?

A perennial question that every investor has regarding BTC is whether it's going to crash anytime soon. There is no easy way to answer this. BTC is far more volatile than any other assets partly because no one fully understands its future in the world economy. There are large speculative forces operating in the currency and this tends to exaggerate price moves.

The volatility in BTC has been one of the things that has scared away institutions in the past. Since 2009, here are some of the volatility events it has undergone:

- 10 drawdowns of over 30%
- 5 drawdowns of over 50%
- 3 drawdowns of over 80%
- 1 drawdown of over 90%

The median drawdown lasts 55 days and reaches an average drop of 35%. The three longest drawdowns lasted an average of 201 days and reached an average drop of 43%. These are much higher than anything that the stock market is used to experiencing. To put it into perspective, a drawdown of 30% (which is the most common large drawdown percentage that BTC experiences) is double the threshold beyond which a hedge fund decides to shut its doors.

Institutional managers who suffer drawdowns of greater than five percent witness a mass exodus. If they suffer a drawdown of 15% or more, they simply shutter their shop since there's no way a traditional asset can recover from those lows in a reasonable period of time. To account for BTC's extreme volatility, portfolio managers have to limit their holdings in it to a small percentage of their overall portfolio.

The other factor that makes BTC impossible to predict is that we have just 11 years' worth of data to work with. Compare this to the stock market that has over a century's worth of data and you can see why so many BTC market participants experience extreme volatility in the short term.

Our advice remains the same as always. Focus on the long-term benefits of the asset and ignore short-term gyrations. In the short term, BTC is driven by extremely emotional forces, mostly of the get-rich-quick type, who want to pile into something that is going to "guarantee" them riches. Long-term investors must note that each drawdown in BTC is different from the previous one. This is because the nature of market participants is ever-evolving leading to constant behavior changes in the market. The reasons for the fluctuation change but one constant remains: BTC is going to experience massive volatility moving forward. For this reason, we strongly recommend an automated purchase approach to take advantage of dollar cost averaging. We have a video tutorial for how to do this in the Bitcoin 101 bonus section.

That being said, if you're someone that cannot stomach extreme volatility in your financial assets, then it's best to stay away from Bitcoin.

FREEMAN BITCOIN INVESTING RULE #10

DRAWDOWNS ARE INEVITABLE AS A BITCOIN INVESTOR. IF YOU CAN'T HANDLE 30% DIPS IN YOUR HOLDINGS, DON'T BUY BITCOIN

OTHER CRYPTOCURRENCIES

What about other cryptocurrencies? While BTC is extremely volatile and has high prices, other cryptos are priced quite low and this makes volatility easier to stomach. After all, there is a big difference in monitoring something priced at $30,000 moving by 30% versus something priced $1.50 that moves 100%.

Altcoin (any cryptocurrency other than BTC) investing has been a trending topic for a few years now thanks to BTC's rise. Once you start reading up about BTC, you'll quickly run into articles that promise to help you find "The next Bitcoin". You will read about altcoins that are poised to rise over the next year whose gains will dwarf those of behemoths like Amazon, Netflix, etc.

The problem with altcoins is that almost all of them are worthless. There are many altcoins that are still fraudulent operations, with people piling money into them due to ignorance. Every time BTC's price rises, you will witness a bunch of no-name coins rising 2,000% or more because no one has a clue about these altcoins.

The only exception to this dismal altcoin situation is Ethereum (ETH). ETH was one of the first altcoins to appear after BTC and it has the same rigorous standards that underlie BTC. In fact, from a technical perspective, many cryptocurrency evangelists consider ETH a more robust currency. After all, the creators of ETH had the opportunity to study BTC and resolve some of its flaws. ETH has a number of real-world use cases and is at the center of the fight to create a decentralized financial system. However, outside of ETH, the picture gets gloomy really fast.

One of the big issues with altcoins is that not all of them are decentralized. This is something that many crypto speculators neglect. A currency's protocols are established by its founders. If the founder chooses to create a Big Brother-type oversight network in the currency, they are free to do so. However, just because a currency functions over the blockchain, doesn't mean it's decentralized.

A good example of this is XRP, or Ripple, as it's traditionally known. This network is meant to facilitate payments around the world and decentralization has nothing to do with its primary aims. It's fully controlled by a company and network users have to play by their rules.

One of the reasons many speculators push money into altcoins is that they behave like penny stocks. Many altcoins trade for less than a dollar. If an altcoin trading at 50 cents rises to $1, that's a 100% gain. Given the volatility that cryptos experience, many speculators see this scenario as a foregone conclusion. The problem is that these altcoins are vulnerable to manipulation. The old stock market tactic of sending newsletters or "trade signals" hyping penny stocks and then dumping them onto gullible investors is still alive in the crypto market. Something you should always remember is that most of these coins don't have anything fundamental backing them.

To cite the most recent example of this, we looked at Dogecoin (pronounced dohj-coin). The internet's favorite meme cryptocurrency was created as a joke that was meant to highlight how ridiculous crypto speculation was becoming. Dogecoin typically gains value whenever there's a bull run at BTC despite the fact that it has zero utility and the founders make no bones about it.

However, these days it has a market cap of over $5 billion dollars, making it larger than many well-known stock market names like Upwork, AMC, Yelp and Sonos.

Figure 9 illustrates how ridiculous speculative pressure can be. You might be tempted to think you can enter and exit on time and make a killing, but this is exactly the sort of attitude that gets you burned.

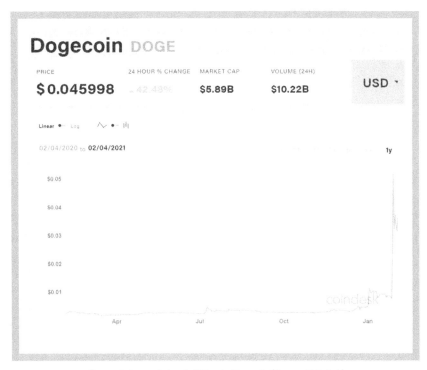

Figure 9: A speculative Bull Run in Dogecoin (Source: Coindesk)

Examining altcoin performance since the previous bull run in BTC is instructive. The best example of that is Nano (or RaiBlocks, as it was previously called). On November 1, 2017, the currency was trading for 10 cents. Fast forward to January 5, 2018, and it was worth $36.01, an astonishing increase of over 35,000% in just two months. Alas, this newfound publicity didn't do Nano any good. The exchange it was trading on was hacked and roughly $200 million worth of Nano went missing. At present, Nano is trading at around $3 per coin.

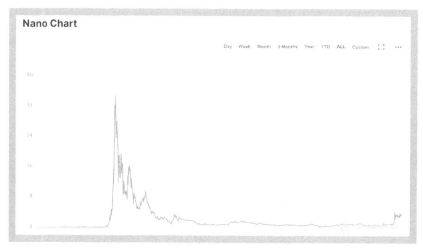

Figure 10: The rise and fall of Nano between 2017 and 2021 (Source: CoinMarketCap)

Ripple was another cryptocurrency which made waves in 2017 during the last bull run. It rose by roughly 30,000% during that time but has dropped 80% since then. The team behind Ripple was sanctioned by the SEC in December 2020 for an illegal securities offering.

Here are some other examples (based on trading values on February 1st 2021):

- Ambrosus – 99.9% down from all time high

- Wanchain - 95% down from all time high
- Dash - 92% down from all time high
- OmiseGo (OMG Network) - 90% down from all time high
- Monero – 72% down from all time high
- Cardano – 64% down from all time high
- Stellar – 63% down from all time high
- Litecoin – 59% down from all time high

But, what about BTC?

Well, in 2017, it gained 1,318% and since then it has gained an additional 68%. Clearly, its underlying fundamentals are far better than those of other cryptocurrencies. BTC's network effect and first mover advantage is truly unassailable.

CONCLUSION

BTC is poised to become this century's gold. While there is no telling how far it will rise or how relevant it will be 100 years from now, there is no doubt that we are on the cusp of discovering a new asset class. Many investors will have safety concerns and to help you understand all the points made in this book, here are the 10 commandments of a safe BTC experience.

#1 - DON'T INVEST IF DRAWDOWNS SCARE YOU

BTC is volatile, extremely so. Drawdowns of 30% or more are considered normal. If the thought of losing 30% in unrealized losses scares you, and if this much volatility causes you to lose sleep at night, then it's best to stay away from investing in BTC. After all, there's no rule that says you have to invest in BTC to make money. There are equally good assets out there that you can place your money in. Investing in crypto because it's the hot thing or because of FOMO is never a good way to navigate your investment operations.

#2 - USE REPUTABLE EXCHANGES

Cryptocurrency investment requires you to understand storage needs and evaluate the technical capabilities of exchanges. Even if you withdraw your holdings to your wallet regularly, you'll still have to place your coins with the exchange's wallet for a certain period of time. A hack or security breach can result in you losing all your gains. The best thing to do is to use only reputable exchanges such as Coinbase, Binance, or Gemini. Do not venture outside these three and you'll be just fine.

#3 - USE A HARDWARE WALLET

Always withdraw your coins to your wallet and don't leave them lying around on the exchange for any longer than necessary. Don't use online wallets or paper wallets because those can be easily compromised. Think of your wallet as being your bank. Secure your wallet the same way a bank secures your money.

#4 - FOLLOW BEST PRACTICES FOR SECURITY

We've outlined some best practices in Chapter 7 that you should follow when securing your coins. Make sure you review these tips and follow them at all times. At the very least, understand the difference between your private and public keys and remember to never divulge your private key information. Be wary of anyone who tries to coerce you into giving them your private key for whatever reason. There is no application of the blockchain that requires another party to have access to your private key.

#5 - ALWAYS ASSUME BITCOIN EMAIL DOWNLOADS ARE SCAMS

The crypto space is very young and unsophisticated. This means regulation is yet to catch up to it, and scammers try various tricks to lure people into traps. A common scam is to email people who own hardware wallets, compelling them to download software to patch or upgrade.

These emails will be sent from domains that closely match the wallet manufacturer's so it can be tough to spot scams. However, most hardware wallets don't need software updates. There have been exceptions where major security flaws have been discovered in them and updates have been sent out. These incidents are well publicized, so it's easy to verify whether the update is genuine or not. It is best to assume that all emails you receive regarding updates to your wallet are fraudulent.

#6 - STAY AWAY FROM ICOS

An ICO is the crypto version of an IPO. While IPOs are conducted under rigorous regulatory frameworks, ICOs employ a Wild West phenomenon and have almost no regulation to them. Most coins that offer ICOs are founded in offshore tax havens that impose zero oversight for the process. We've already spoken about how fraudulent coins are launched. It's best to stay away from ICOs and let someone else take the risk.

#7 - STAY AWAY FROM CLOUD MINING OPERATIONS

Mining by itself is an unprofitable operation. To invest in a cloud mining operation, where you pay someone money to mine coins for you and store them, is a particularly risky thing to do. It's best to stick to investing in BTC directly through reputable exchanges.

#8 - STAY AWAY FROM LENDING PROGRAMS

If there's a dead giveaway that a crypto offering is fraudulent, it's a lending program attached to it. The economics of cryptocurrency ensure that a lending program can never work. Therefore, anyone who promises you steady returns on your investment in cash, like rent on a piece of real estate, is almost certainly perpetrating fraud. Stay away from these.

9 - DON'T SPECULATE IN CRYPTOCURRENCIES

Our counsel has always been to invest in BTC and stay away from other cryptocurrencies. We also advise you to invest long term and not fall prey to speculation. This is easier said than done since you will routinely read about some altcoin or the other gaining over 20% in just a few days because Elon Musk thinks it's the next big thing. Remain focused and always act according to the investment principles we've outlined in this book and our other books. They're certain to make you money, as long as you remain patient.

10 – ENJOY YOURSELF

Most importantly, BTC should be a "nice to have" bonus in your portfolio rather than your entire livelihood. It is 5-10% of your portfolio which in a best case scenario could balloon to 50% or more. So, don't stress yourself out by checking prices every day, or overreacting to social media posts every time it dips below $40,000.

Like it or not, Bitcoin is here to stay, but as we've explained through this book, it doesn't have to be complicated. Make it a point to refer to this book whenever you have any doubts.

Alternatively, you can email us at admin@freemanpublications.com if you would like something clarified. We answer every single reader email.

2020 was a chaotic year, and as we move into 2021, we wish you the best of luck with your investing!

One final word from us. If this book has helped you in any way, we'd appreciate it if you left us a review on Amazon. Reviews are the lifeblood of our business. We read every single one and incorporate your feedback into our future book projects.

To leave an Amazon review, go to

https://freemanpublications.com/leaveareview

"THE MOST SUCCESSFUL PEOPLE IN LIFE ARE THE ONES WHO
ASK QUESTIONS. THEY'RE ALWAYS LEARNING. THEY'RE
ALWAYS GROWING. THEY'RE ALWAYS PUSHING."

- Robert Kiyosaki

CONTINUING YOUR JOURNEY

Like Robert Kiyosaki said on the previous page, "The most successful people in life are always learning, growing, and asking questions."

Which is why we created our investing community, aptly named *How To NOT Lose Money in the Stock Market*, so that like-minded individuals could get together to share ideas and learn from each other.

We regularly run giveaways, share wins from our readers, and you'll be the first to know when our new books are released.

It's 100% free, and there are no requirements to join, except for the willingness to learn.

You can join us on Facebook by going to

http://freemanpublications.com/facebook

OTHER BOOKS BY FREEMAN PUBLICATIONS (AVAILABLE ON AMAZON & AUDIBLE)

The 8-Step Beginner's Guide to Value Investing: Featuring 20 for 20 - The 20 Best Stocks & ETFs to Buy and Hold for The Next 20 Years

Bear Market Investing Strategies: 37 Recession-Proof Ideas to Grow Your Wealth - Including Inverse ETFs, Put Options, Gold & Cryptocurrency

Iron Condor Options for Beginners: A Smart, Safe Method to Generate an Extra 25% Per Year with Just 2 Trades Per Month

COVERED
CALLS
—— for ——
BEGINNERS

A RISK-FREE WAY TO COLLECT
"RENTAL INCOME" EVERY SINGLE MONTH ON
STOCKS YOU ALREADY OWN

FREEMAN PUBLICATIONS

Covered Calls for Beginners: A Risk-Free Way to Collect "Rental Income" Every Single Month on Stocks You Already Own

CREDIT
SPREAD
OPTIONS
—— for ——
BEGINNERS

TURN YOUR MOST BORING STOCKS INTO
RELIABLE MONTHLY PAYCHECKS
using
CALL, PUT & IRON BUTTERFLY SPREADS
EVEN IF THE MARKET IS DOING NOTHING

FREEMAN PUBLICATIONS

Credit Spread Options for Beginners: Turn Your Most Boring Stocks into Reliable Monthly Paychecks using Call, Put & Iron Butterfly Spreads - Even If The Market is Doing Nothing

Featuring The 13 Best High Yield Stocks,
REITs, MLPs and CEFs for Retirement Income

DIVIDEND
GROWTH
INVE$TING

GET A STEADY 8% PER YEAR
—— Even in ——
A ZERO INTEREST RATE WORLD

FREEMAN PUBLICATIONS

Dividend Growth Investing: Get a Steady 8% Per Year Even in a Zero Interest Rate World - Featuring The 13 Best High Yield Stocks, REITs, MLPs and CEFs For Retirement Income

ACKNOWLEDGMENTS

This book is a team effort, and while I get to be the face of the business and receive all the kind messages from readers, I can't ignore the people who helped make this book what it was.

Thank you first to our content team for their writing, editing, and proofreading efforts and dealing with my persistent questions about why specific changes needed to be made.

Thank you to Mark Greenberg, our superstar narrator, who has really become "the voice" of Freeman Publications over the past year.

Thank you to Ed Fahy over at UBF for always being there every time I needed to make a minor update to the book interior.

Thank you to all Freeman readers who participated in our advanced reader program for this book. Thank you to K, Kimberley, Mark, Erik, Edwin, Andy, Anthony, Rogerio, Wanda, Ryan, Leland, Aster, Stevie, Lewis, Arthur, Len, Kern, Nic, Joanna, Eric, James, Gilbert, Gilbert (again!), Jacqueline, Patrick, Tatee and Erik (again!)

Thank you to Alex for fact checking the technical aspects of our Bitcoin coverage.

Thank you to our hundreds of readers on social media for your words of encouragement throughout this project.

Finally, thank you to my family, whose initial uncertainty of "are you still doing that book thing" has blossomed into full support for my vision here at Freeman Publications. This means more than you will ever know.

Oliver

London, England

February, 2021

REFERENCES

10 Fascinating Amazon Statistics Sellers Need To Know in 2019. (2019, February 8). The BigCommerce Blog. https://www.bigcommerce.-com/blog/amazon-statistics/#:~:text=In%202018%2C%20Amazon

Bartlett, J. (2019, November 14). "Cryptoqueen" brother admits role in OneCoin fraud. *BBC News*. https://www.bbc.com/news/technology-50417908

Bitclub. (2019, December 9). Www.Justice.Gov. https://www.justice.gov/usao-nj/bitclub

Borate, N. (2021, January 11). *What is bitcoin halving and will it affect the rate?* Mint. https://www.livemint.com/money/personal-finance/what-is-bitcoin-halving-and-will-it-affect-the-rate-11610295621496.html

Canadian in Dubai Arrested for Fraud, Including Crypto Fraud via Habibi Coin, the "Bitcoin of the Middle East." (2019, November 3). Crowdfund Insider. https://www.crowdfundinsider.com/2019/11/153580-

canadian-in-dubai-arrested-for-fraud-including-crypto-fraud-via-habibi-coin-the-bitcoin-of-the-middle-east

Goyette, B. (2011, January 20). *Cheat Sheet: What's Happened to the Big Players in the Financial Crisis.* ProPublica. https://www.propublica.org/article/cheat-sheet-whats-happened-to-the-big-players-in-the-financial-crisis#:~:text=According%20to%20the%20Financial%20Crisis

IRS Bank Levies Can Take Your Money. (2014, September 18). Debt.com. https://www.debt.com/tax-debt/irs-bank-levy/#:~:text=The%20IRS%20can%20remove%20money

Kagan, J. (2019). *Income Tax Definition.* Investopedia. https://www.investopedia.com/terms/i/incometax.asp

Lyanchev, J. (2020, November 16). *Bitcoin Price to Reach $318K by December 2021 as the New Gold, Citibank Director Says.* CryptoPotato. https://cryptopotato.com/bitcoin-price-to-reach-318k-by-december-2021-as-the-new-gold-citibank-director-says/#:~:text=Citibank%20Director%20Says-

Nytimes.com. 2021. *Bitcoin Has Lost Steam. But Criminals Still Love It. (Published 2020).* [online] Available at: https://www.nytimes.com/2020/01/28/technology/bitcoin-black-market.html

Redman, J. (2020). *This is How Much BTC You Need to Enter Bitcoin's Elite 1% Club* (Published 2020). Bitcoin.com https://news.bitcoin.com/this-is-how-much-btc-you-need/

Roberts, J. (2020). *To Catch a Bitcoin Thief, Call These Detectives.* Fortune. http://fortune.com/2018/06/27/bitcoin-detective-zcash-cryptocurrency/

Sharma, V. (2020). *Will 2021 Be the Year When India Finally Clarifies Laws Around Cryptocurrencies?* The Wire. https://thewire.in/tech/will-

2021-be-the-year-when-india-finally-clarifies-laws-around-cryptocurrencies

Swift.com. 2021. [online] Available at: <https://www.swift.com/sites/default/files/files/swift_bae_report_Follow-The%20Money.pdf>

Virtual Currencies. (2014). Irs.Gov. https://www.irs.gov/businesses/small-businesses-self-employed/virtual-currencies

Made in the USA
Las Vegas, NV
22 November 2024

12415686R00073